PEACE OR ARMAGEDDON?

The Unfolding Drama of the Middle East Peace Accord

Dan O'Neill & Don Wagner

Foreword by Richard C. Halverson

ZondervanPublishingHouse
Grand Rapids, Michigan

A Division of HarperCollins*Publishers*

*To the victims of violence, terrorism, and military occupation
on both sides of this most complex and protracted conflict:
the Jews of Israel and the Arabs of Palestine.*

*May peace with justice bring a new day
to you and to your children.*

*And to the church of the Middle East,
may God grant you hope that is built on
the secure foundation of love, truth, and God's justice.*

PEACE OR ARMAGEDDON?
The Unfolding Drama of the Middle East Peace Accord
Copyright © 1993 Dan O'Neill and Don Wagner
All rights reserved.

Requests for information should be addressed to:
Zondervan Publishing House
Grand Rapids, Michigan 49530

Library of Congress Cataloging-in-Publication Data

ISBN 0-310-44401-2

Edited by Lyn Cryderman
Cover design by John M. Lucas
Cover photo by Wide World Photos, Inc.

93 94 95 96 97 / CH / 7 6 5 4 3 2 1

Key Terms in This Book

ALLAH: The word for God used by Arabic-speaking Christians and Muslims.

ANTICHRIST: According to certain fundamentalist Christians and based on selected passages of Daniel and Revelation, the term applied to an evil latter-day world ruler, who will rise against Israel and the forces of good only to be defeated by the Second Coming of Jesus Christ and the armies of God.

ARMAGEDDON: The site of the final battle of history, according to the fundamentalist end-time theology; the actual site is the Valley of Megiddo in central Israel.

BALFOUR DECLARATION: The November 1917 letter from British Foreign Secretary Lord Arthur Balfour to Baron Lionel Rothschild, announcing that "His Majesty's Government views with favour the establishment in Palestine of a national home for the Jewish people . . . it being clearly understood that nothing shall be done which may prejudice the civil and religious rights of existing non-Jewish communities in Palestine." The Declaration granted to the Zionist movement their initial legitimacy.

COPTIC: The Christians of Egypt (Orthodox, Catholic, and Evangelical) numbering approximately eight million.

DISPENSATIONALISM: A system of Christian theology that divides history into epochs (usually 5–7) according to God's relationship to humanity. It is generally a belief system that concentrates on prophecies concerning the end of history.

ERETZ YISRAEL: Hebrew for "greater Israel," or all of Palestine; the political vision for the right-wing parties of Israel.

HOLOCAUST: Literally, "a sacrifice consumed by fire," also applies to the destruction of a particular ethnic or racial group. The term is usually applied to the genocidal suffering of the Jewish people during the Nazi era.

HOLY LAND: The land of Israel and Palestine, with historic sites, traditions, and people, sacred to Islam, Judaism, and Christianity.

3

I.D.F.: The initials for the Israeli Defense Forces, the army of the state of Israel.

INTIFADA: The popular uprising of the Palestinian people inside the occupied Palestinian territories beginning in 1987; literally, "the shaking off" in Arabic.

KNESSET: The 120-member Parliament of Israel, located in Jerusalem.

LABOR PARTY: The bloc of parties that founded Israel and ruled from 1948–77 and again after 1992, composed largely of European Jewry.

LIKUD: The right-wing block of ideologically motivated parties that led to the Government of Israel from 1977–92.

MIDDLE EAST COUNCIL OF CHURCHES (MECC): The eumenical umbrella that today includes twelve to fourteen million Christians. Oriental and Eastern Orthodox, Catholic, and Protestant (Evangelical) churches comprise the council.

MUSLIM (Islam): "One who submits" to Allah, the religion begun by the Prophet Muhammad in the seventh century A.C.E.

AL-NAKHBAH: "The catastrophe" in Arabic; applies to the forced expulsion of 700,000-to-760,000 Palestinians from their land and homes by Israel in 1948–49, beginning the Palestinian refugee crisis.

PARTITION: The United Nations General Assembly vote of November 29, 1947, to divide Palestine into a Jewish and Arab (Palestinian) state, rejected by the Arabs because of the demographic nuances that favored the Zionists.

QUR'AN (Koran): Literally, "recitation" in Arabic; the messages from God (Allah) to the Prophet Muhammad, recorded by his followers to form the Holy Scriptures of Islam.

SEMITE (Semitic): Originally a linguistic term that referred to the languages of the Middle Eastern people of the Eastern Mediterranean, later applied to the people who spoke Arabic, Hebrew, Syriac, Aramaic, and other languages.

TORAH: The first five books of Moses, also called the Pentateuch and known in Judaism as the Law.

ZIONISM: The political movement begun in Europe during the late nineteenth century to establish for the Jewish people a national homeland with international legitimacy. The term comes from "Zion"—the mountain in Jerusalem that sits at the Dome of the Rock and previously in Jewish temples.

Contents

Part I

What Happened?
by Don Wagner

Part II

What Could Still Happen in the Holy Land
by Dan O'Neill

Part III

What It Means
by Dan O'Neill and Don Wagner

Foreword

by Richard C. Halverson, Chaplain
United States Senate

After centuries of controversy and conflict, a handshake at the White House opened the door to peace in the Middle East.

The following pages offer a first-hand report on the handshake, its promises, and its problems. Written by two men who have a long history of involvement in the Israeli-Palestinian situation, who have been deeply concerned for peace in the Middle East, and who are thoroughly and intimately acquainted with Scripture, this book is required reading.

As the authors write, they give a knowledgeable record of the history of the tragedy and the suffering of the Jews as well as the Palestinians. To many Western Christians, it comes as a surprise that a large number of Palestinians profess faith in Christ and that the history of that faith goes all the way back to Pentecost.

It is not uncommon to meet Palestinian believers who are very conscious of their history and who feel abandoned by their sisters and brothers in Europe, the United States, and Canada. The uncritical support for Israel by many Western evangelists unintentionally communicates this bias.

Praying for the peace of Jerusalem *must* include the Palestinians. This discussion of the current situation will do much to enlighten those unfamiliar with the Middle East, and at the same time it will encourage our sisters and brothers in Palestine. As we pray for the peace of Jerusalem, let us pray for all who love this city that is so intimately connected to biblical faith.

Preface

T wenty years ago I was a photographer living in northern Israel at Kibbutz Ginosar on the Sea of Galilee. I witnessed and photographed live shelling, tank battles, and aerial combat during the sudden attack on Israel by Syria and Egypt. The intensity of the battle was frightening, and I was worried about the nation I loved: Israel, God's chosen people.

I learned later that when Israel was pressed against the wall and its very existence was threatened by the attacking Arabs, it contemplated using nuclear weapons to defend itself. Few people know how close Damascus came to incineration that night.

The terror of battle and the horrible thought of Israel's using nuclear weapons began for me a long process of reflection and concern about events in the Middle East. I began to question my own undying support for Israel as I continued to work on the kibbutz after the war and saw how the people I loved, my Jewish friends, utterly hated the Palestinian laborers who performed menial tasks on the kibbutz. It reminded me of what I had seen the year before on a visit to South Africa, where I stayed in the homes of respected Christian families who treated black South Africans with the same disdain."

A subsequent jolt came in 1978, when I joined a small delegation of Christian leaders who were the guests of Prime Minister Menachem Begin. I had been made aware of the

9

antimissionary bill that passed the Knesset on Christmas Day 1977, making illegal any evangelization or proselytizing activities of Jews in Israel. I am an evangelical Christian who loves Israel, but I had to ask Mr. Begin the obvious question: "How could you allow this bill to pass when we Christians in the United States give you so much support?" The prime minister looked at his aides and angrily asked in Hebrew: "Who let this person in to ask these kinds of questions?" Knowing Hebrew fluently, I was troubled by his response.

Meanwhile, at the very moment I was in the bomb shelter on the Sea of Galilee, my coauthor, Don Wagner, was driving from the East Coast to Chicago to begin a new pastorate. He recalls following the news carefully as he drove that first week in October 1973. "I was really worried about Israel and found myself praying constantly for God's people, the Jews, to be spared during this war."

Three months earlier Don had been in Auschwitz, leading thirty-five high school and college youth on a study tour to Europe, a study that concentrated on the Holocaust, the church in Eastern Europe, and Christian responsibility. "I will never forget my visit to Auschwitz as long as I live," Don reflects. "The bins of baby pacifiers, the artificial limbs from Nazi experiments on Jews, the lampshades made of human skin, and then the gas ovens. I was speechless when I left. I gathered our entire group of thirty-five in the parking lot, and we bowed our heads to pray silently. That was all we could do."

During the winter of 1974, Don and several lay leaders organized a study course on the Middle East at his new church. As a loyal friend of Israel and one committed to Zionism, Don made certain that over 50 percent of the presenters faithfully argued the case of Israel. But he also invited a seminarian who had helped settle Palestinian refugees during 1949–50. "That was the first time I heard an articulate Palestinian Christian who presented his case persuasively and factually. Up to this point I had viewed Palestinians only as terrorists and enemies of Israel." Halfway through the course Don received a disturbing phone call from a person who described himself as a Holocaust survivor, who said he would picket the church if the course was not stopped immediately. Don decided to begin reading everything he could about the Middle East conflict to see what was so dangerous about the Palestinian point of view.

Two years later, as part of the newly formed Middle East Task Force of the Chicago Presbytery, his group brought five Christian leaders from the Middle East to Chicago: a Palestinian theologian, two Lebanese Christian leaders, a Coptic (Egyptian) bishop, and a theologian. They asked Don point-blank: "Why have you Western Christians abandoned the Christians of the Middle East? It is okay if you support Israel, but at the expense of justice for both Jews and Palestinians? Why should we have to pay the price for anti-Semitism when it is fundamentally a Western problem? You Westerners did not allow Jews to enter your nations, so you solved the Jewish question at the expense of the Palestinians."

In 1982, Don and I met for the first time in Beirut, Lebanon. We were part of a fact-finding team for Mercy Corps International, a Christian relief agency I had helped organize. Within five days of our arrival, Israel launched a ferocious bombardment of the city, just eight short blocks from our hotel. Kneeling in the basement of the Beau Rivage Hotel, we prayed desperately for safety as block-buster bombs shook the foundations of the hotel and wreaked massive destruction and killed many civilians nearby. We would never be the same, because now we knew

there was another suffering people—the Palestinians—
whose story had not been told to the West.

We write this book not as pro-Palestinians or pro-Israelis
but as Christians who love both the peoples and have
personally met and worked with their leaders. Our goal is to
help others understand the need for these two nations to
find ways to live peacefully with each other. We believe that
at this point in history it is indeed in God's plan that the
killing and destruction stop.

This is not an in-depth political analysis, a historical
survey of the conflict, nor a theological treatise. However,
we have talked with many who were close to the secret
negotiations between Israel and the PLO and will share some
of this behind-the-scenes information. We have drawn from
our experience in that region to suggest what might happen
in the days to come. And we have interviewed scores of
Christian leaders to help us understand how this historic
agreement fits into God's design.

We understand that Christians have varying interpretations of prophecy that influence their views of Israel and her
neighbors. Even Don and I have our own disagreement on
these important questions, but we find common ground in
our commitment to the Gospel and our calling to be bearers
of Good News to all people. It is our hope that this brief
look at one of the most important developments in the Holy
Land will unleash a torrent of prayer for the peace of all of
Jerusalem and the surrounding countryside that may one day
be the home of two nations, Israel and Palestine.

Dan O'Neill
Seattle, Washington
October 12, 1993

Acknowledgments

Any project of this scope and limited time frame requires a team effort, upheld by God's grace. We are thankful that both of these elements were present as we labored against incredibly tight deadlines.

First, we thank Mercy Corps International staff in our Portland, Redmond, and Chicago offices. Our Resource Development Director, Ron Frey, and Middle East Regional Director, Lowell Ewert, were a critical part of our team. Ells Culver, president, was most supportive and encouraging. Special mention must be made of Melinda Harvey and Skye Leslie for their word-processing skills. Susanne Donoghue was incredible in editing and beating tough deadlines. Eleanor Ehresman and Lynn Offtick of First Presbyterian Church, Evanston, Illinois, helped meet a critical deadline with the first draft of the manuscript.

The hospitality and support of our friends at Loyola Retreat Center in Portland, Oregon, is deeply appreciated.

Special research assistance was provided by Peter Lems of the International Office of the Palestine Human Rights Information Center in Washington, D.C. We also received valuable editorial insights from a Palestinian American political scientist and a Jewish historian, both of whom asked for no acknowledgements—but we know you and thank you. Landrum Bolling, Senior Fellow, Harvard University's School of Conflict Management, a friend of both Israeli and Palestinian leaders and a true peacemaker, offered invaluable editorial suggestions, as did Dr. Mubarak Awad, Director of Non-Violence International.

We could not imagine a more visionary and affirming editor than Lyn Cryderman. This book could not have been written without his remarkable skills. Thank you.

Finally, we thank our families, the O'Neills and the Wagners, especially our wives, who tolerated long hours and absence from the home.

To all our Israeli and Palestinian friends we extend our hopes and prayers for peace, knowing that this accord is a small beginning. The difficult work of peacemaking and healing still lies before us. If we have understated or overemphasized certain issues, the mistakes are ours. Please read this modest contribution to the cause, knowing that we will continue to stand with you in building new societies based on justice.

Dan O'Neill and Don Wagner
October 15, 1993

Part I

What Happened?

by Don Wagner

UN PARTITION PLAN – 1947
AND
UN ARMISTICE LINES – 1949

———·—— Boundary of Former Palestine Mandate

PLAN OF PARTITION, 1947

Arab State
Jewish State
Jerusalem

——— Armistice Demarcation lines, 1949
(Shown where at variance with Mandate boundary.)

LEBANON

Tyre

o Quneitra

Nahariyya

GOLAN

SYRIA

Acre

Safad

o Nawa

Haifa

Lake
Tiberias

Shef'at'am

Tiberias

Nazareth

Hadera

Jenin

Netanya

Tulkarm

Kefar Sava

Qalqilya

Nablus

Tel Aviv

WEST

Arab

Jaffa

BANK

Rishon Le Zion

Jordan

Ramle

Ramallah

o Amman

Rehovot

Laitun

Jericho

Jerusalem

o Bethlehem

MEDITERRANEAN

SEA

Hebron

Dead
Sea

JORDAN

Gaza

GAZA

Khan Yunis

Rafah

Beersheba

o El Arish

ISRAEL

SINAI

EGYPT

Elat

Gulf of
Aqaba

LEBANON

ISRAEL

SYRIA

Tel Aviv

Jerusalem

JORDAN

EGYPT

0   10   20   30km
0   10   20   30mi

*The designations employed and the presentation of
material on this map do not imply the expression of
any opinion whatsoever on the part of the Secretariat
of the United Nations concerning the legal status of
any country, territory, city or area or of its authorities, or
concerning the delimitation of its frontiers or boundaries.*

0   30km
0   30mi

MAP NO. 3067   UNITED NATIONS
SEPTEMBER 1979

1

The Handshake That Shocked the World

It was a perfect September day in Washington, D.C. By 11:00 A.M. the sun was shining brightly out of a deep blue sky as the temperature climbed into the high 80s. Thousands were gathering on the south lawn of the White House fully conscious that they were about to witness a remarkable historical moment. A massive army of reporters and cameramen were there to cover the event while sharpshooters monitored every inch of real estate. The proceedings would be watched in over one hundred nations around the world.

A few minutes after 11:00 A.M., the introductions began as the dignitaries strolled to their places:

> Ladies and gentlemen, the Vice-President of the United States, Albert Gore, Jr.; His Excellency, Shimon Peres, Minister of Foreign Affairs of Israel; Mr. Abbas, Member of the Executive Council of the Palestine Liberation Organization.

Sustained applause followed as Secretary of State Warren Christopher and the Russian Federation's Minister of Foreign Affairs Andrei Kozyrev emerged from the White House.

Then came a prolonged moment of anticipation as everyone realized that the three major players in this drama were about to be introduced: "Ladies and gentlemen, Mr.

Arafat, chairman of the Executive Council (his correct title is chairman of the Executive Committee of the Palestine National Council, of the Palestine Liberation Organization); His Excellency, Yitzhak Rabin, prime minister of Israel; the President of the United States."

The wild applause was punctured with frequent high-pitched whistles and cheers, not the usual fare at such occasions. President Clinton strolled to the platform, flanked by Rabin on his right and Arafat on his left. The impossible was beginning to happen.

For nearly one hundred years Jews and Arabs, and Palestinians in particular, have been locked in an escalating cycle of seemingly irreconcilable hostilities. As late as Friday, September 10, serious conflicts remained, threatening twenty months of tedious, secret negotiations. The Israelis planned to send Foreign Minister Shimon Peres to sign the document. They believed that the Palestinian side would send Abu-Mazen, PLO Executive Committee member and head of the political department that supervised the secret negotiations.

At 7:00 P.M. Friday evening the Palestinians told the State Department that Chairman Arafat would head their delegation and Abu-Mazen would accompany him. *TIME* magazine reported that the State Department's special coordinator of Middle East policy, Dennis Ross, then called Warren Christopher, who was having drinks with reporters at his house in Georgetown. Christopher ducked into a side room and called the president. Worried that Arafat's involvement might create problems, the two agreed to keep the request quiet until they informed Rabin first thing in the morning.

Shortly after midnight Christopher called Rabin who had, to nobody's surprise, already learned of the PLO's request. His response: "If he is coming, I have no other alternative. I'll come." (*TIME* magazine, September 20, 1993).

This confirmed what I had heard in Washington, D.C. on Friday. "According to our people in Tunis," a PLO executive and friend, Jiryis Atrash, a Christian from Bethlehem, stated, "Abu-Ammar (Arafat's *nom de guerre*) is definitely coming. It is only for the State Department to work out a few minor details. The deal is done."

"Impossible!" I replied. "You've got to believe in miracles," he added with a twinkle in his eye. Remarkably, like the entire secret negotiation process, the U.S. government vaulted decades of official prohibitions banning contact with the PLO and the path was cleared for Arafat's arrival.

President Clinton moved to the microphone. The *Washington Post* reported that he had awakened at approximately 3:00 A.M. that day, unable to sleep because he felt that his speech needed more work. He reached for his Bible and reread the entire book of Joshua and portions of the New Testament. His opening words echoed both his Christian faith and a heightened sense of history:

> Welcome to this great occasion of history and hope. Today, we bear witness to an extraordinary act in one of history's defining dramas, a drama that began in a time of our ancestors when the Word went forth from a sliver of land between the River Jordan and the Mediterranean

Sea. That hallowed piece of earth, that land of life and
revelation is the home to the memories and dreams of
Jews, Muslims, and Christians throughout the world.

The president's use of biblical imagery set the tone for
his address, an interesting mixture of hope and political
realism. But it should be noted that Clinton's initial reaction
to news of the secret PLO-Israeli accord two weeks earlier
was cynical and far from encouraging. According to press
reports, the president expressed doubts that the secret
negotiations would produce anything new. Now, however,
he was obviously pleased to host this historic event.

"A brave peace is within our reach," he noted.
"Throughout the Middle East, there is a great yearning for
the quiet miracle of a normal life." He surprised many
listeners by interjecting that the "Koran teaches that if the
enemy inclines toward peace, do thou also incline toward
peace." He noted how centuries earlier, Jews and Muslims
once lived together and wrote "brilliant chapters in the
history of literature and science. All this can come to pass
again." A thunderous applause affirmed his words.

Then Clinton pledged what had been missing from the
previous twenty-two months of the frustrating Madrid peace
process: "the active support of the United States of America
to the difficult work that lies ahead." No doubt, members of
Congress squirmed as Arafat and Rabin nodded their heads
in approval.

The United States is committed to ensuring that the
people who are affected by this agreement will be made
more secure by it, and to leading the world in marshaling
the resources necessary to implement the difficult details
that will make real the principles to which you commit
yourselves today . . . Mr. Prime Minister, Mr. Chairman,

this day belongs to you . . . Together, today, with all our hearts and all our souls, we bid them *shalom, salaam, peace.*

President Clinton's conclusion echoed almost to the word what former President Carter had stated following the signing of the Camp David Accord some thirteen years earlier. Clinton's mood reflected a mixture of Baptist homiletics and careful political thought, affirming each major player and religion without unnecessarily offending mainstream opposition.

Prime Minister Rabin, obviously uncomfortable with his forced companionship with avowed enemy Yasser Arafat, took the microphone and brought hushed laughter when he admitted in classic Jewish understatement: "This signing of the Israeli-Palestinian declaration of principles here today, it's not so easy." Then he struck a more somber tone, noting the pain that the Holocaust inflicted on a generation of "families of the victims of the wars, violence, terror, whose pain will never heal. For them, this ceremony has come too late."

But Rabin was characteristically direct when he made two points vital to the Israeli position. First, his unswerving commitment to seize this opportunity for peace:

We who have fought against you, the Palestinians, we say to you today in a loud and a clear voice: Enough of blood and tears. Enough!

But then, to nobody's surprise, he sent a direct shot across Arafat's bow on the issue that for Rabin, is nonnegotiable: "We have come from Jerusalem, *the ancient and eternal capital of the Jewish people.*" That statement is charged with political meaning, as Rabin was claiming Israeli control over all of Jerusalem—forever. It foreshadows the difficult path ahead in resolving the status of a city claimed by both peoples—the city that inspires the religious emotions of all.

Rabin, like Clinton, referred frequently to the Bible, once from the *Koheleth* (Book of Ecclesiastes): "To everything there is a season and a time to every purpose under heaven. . . . Ladies and gentlemen, the time for peace has come." Again, a rousing applause punctured the air. He concluded with a reference to the Jewish New Year, Rosh Hashana, about to begin later that week, hoping it "will bring a message of redemption for all peoples."

Both Rabin and Peres, spoke directly to their points in clear, polished English. Arafat, however, spoke in Arabic with English translation, which seemed to distance many listeners but would be appreciated by the millions of Arabs listening worldwide. His text was exactly the same length as Rabin's, opening with the Islamic greeting, "In the name of God, the most merciful, the compassionate." Arafat greeted President Clinton, to whom he referred on five separate occasions in the speech—clearly Arafat's "target audience." The PLO Chairman then seized the opportunity to address the American public: "We share your values for freedom, justice, and human rights, values for which my people have been striving." He underscored how the Palestinians were now depending on President Clinton and the United States to "usher in an age of peace, coexistence and equal rights."

Then Arafat cited the need to implement all aspects of United Nations Resolutions 242 and 338, a subject that still separates Israeli, American, and Palestinian negotiators. The international consensus (and the official U.S. position since 1967) is that the United Nations resolutions are the basis of "a land in exchange for peace" formula that will bring a just settlement to the Israeli-Palestinian conflict. Israel and the United States have consistently pressed other formulas that fall short of the UN resolutions. Arafat also raised the issues of Jerusalem, settlements, and refugees, signaling Israel and the Americans that the PLO was not satisfied with the lack of definition on these vital issues in the agreement.

His shining moment came when he addressed Israel's security needs:

> Our people do not consider that exercising the right to self-determination could violate the rights of their neighbors or infringe on their security. Rather, putting an end to their feelings of being wronged and of having suffered historic injustices, is the strongest guarantee to achieve coexistence and openness between our two peoples and future generations. Our two peoples are awaiting today this historic hope, and they want to give peace a real chance.

More enthusiastic applause welcomed the chairman's clever appeal.

Then as agreed by all sides, at exactly 11:43 A.M. Eastern Standard Time Shimon Peres and Abu Mazen took turns signing the historic Middle East Accord, a first step on the journey to end the hundred years of conflict.

The next step was more than symbolic. Would they shake hands?

Prime Minister Rabin, when asked in Tel Aviv as he boarded his flight to Washington, hinted that he might not shake Arafat's hand. In a private meeting on Sunday, September 12, for heads of Arab-American organizations, Arafat was asked whether *he* would shake Rabin's hand. He smiled and said, "Why not? Of course I will."

Arafat stepped forward and extended his hand toward Rabin. Two, perhaps three, long seconds elapsed before Rabin hesitantly responded, grasping Arafat's hand. The spectators broke out with cheers and loud applause in affirmation of what they had just witnessed; some wiped tears from their eyes.

Meanwhile on the podium, Arafat also shook the hand of Shimon Peres, while Rabin appeared to chide Peres in Hebrew. What he actually said the world may never know.

2

The Secret Path to Peace

News of an Israeli-PLO agreement began to leak out to the world in the last days of August 1993, on the eve of the tenth round of the U.S.-Soviet sponsored Madrid peace talks. Dissension within the Palestinian delegation saw the head of the delegation, the respected Dr. Haider Abdel-Shafi of Gaza, one of the original founders of the PLO, resign from his role in utter frustration. Prominent members of the PLO submitted their resignations from various posts, some from the Palestine National Council (Palestinian Parliament), demanding Arafat's resignation. At the end of August, the PLO appeared weak, financially and politically bankrupt, and on the verge of a total collapse. On the international scene, Arafat appeared to be finished as his leadership was seriously challenged by the radical Islamic movement *Hamas*.

But another miraculous development was about to emerge, one that would rescue Arafat's credibility and the PLO from collapse. Since the early 1970s, several secret channels had been tested to bring PLO officials into direct negotiations with Israel. Many PLO officials had paid with their lives in political assassinations, while others had died natural deaths or had simply given up. One of the secret channels, the precise details of which were unknown to all but twelve-to-fourteen people in the world, was about to bear fruit.

The drama behind the September 13 accord may be more fascinating than the signature ceremony. Reliable sources close to the PLO report that as the Madrid talks began to bog down after the initial November 1991 session, Nelson Mandela of the African National Congress advised Yasser Arafat to open high-level channels (not necessarily secret) with top Israeli officials. Dr. Mubarak Awad, a Palestinian Christian and director of Non-Violence International, was involved in relaying several early messages from Mandela to Arafat, and vice versa.

The PLO already had several discussions underway with a variety of Israelis, but Mandela's encouragement prompted renewed efforts. In one of the secret channels, according to another Palestinian source, there were very high-level discussions between PLO and Israeli security (Shin Bet) on the issue of internal security. These discussions were independent of the Norway initiative and virtually simultaneous with it. Once the security discussions reached a high level of understanding during the early summer of 1993, the Norway channel was put on a fast track.

The Israeli-PLO process provides drama sufficient for a major docudrama and spy novel. The following narrative sketches out the background. Certainly more details will follow in succeeding months. One aspect of the story began in Tel Aviv in April 1992, when Terje Rod Larsen, director of the Norwegian Institute for Applied Social Science (FAFO) met with a member of the Israeli Knesset (Parliament), Yossi Beilin. Larsen suggested to Beilin, "Would you like to be put in direct contact with senior members of the Palestine Liberation Organization?" Intrigued, Beilin did not accept the offer immediately, nor did he dismiss it.

Meanwhile, the Norwegian Institute had maintained excellent working relationships with various Palestinian leaders in the Occupied Territories and with the PLO itself for several years. In the late 1970s, when Norway maintained a significant detachment of troops in the United Nations forces in southern Lebanon (UNIFIL), then Defense Minister of Norway Johan Jorgen Holst had met with Chairman Arafat and senior PLO leaders on many occasions, negotiating various arrangements in Lebanon. Marianne Heiberg, the defense minister's wife, had authored one of the research papers for FAFO outlining a potential Norwegian role in direct negotiations.

In mid-July 1992, the Israeli Labor party defeated the Likud party, and Yossi Beilin became the deputy foreign minister, reporting directly to Foreign Minister Shimon Peres. Larsen returned to Jerusalem with an expanded agenda that had been cleared previously with high PLO leadership: that the Israelis use Norway as a secret channel for direct negotiations with the PLO. Beilin referred him to Yair Hirschfeld, Professor of Middle East history at Haifa University in Israel.

On September 10, 1992, Larsen returned to Israel with Norwegian State Secretary Jan Egeland, their second senior diplomat. Now the Israelis knew the Norwegians were serious. Meanwhile, FAFO and other Norwegian colleagues had reached secret agreements with Palestinian authorities in Arafat's circle who were willing to pursue the covert channels with Norway. According to the *New York Times* account of the negotiations, Beilin later told associates that while he was fascinated by the Norwegian offer, he was skeptical and put little effort into it for several months. Also, it was essential for Beilin's political career and the Labor Party's future that Beilin refrain from making contact with the PLO. In fact, it was illegal by Israeli law for any citizen of Israel to meet with the PLO, a punishable crime.

The first major threshold was crossed in December 1992, at the Forte Crest St. James Hotel in central London.

Professor Hirschfeld entered the lounge to join Larsen for breakfast. After a cordial but brief conversation, Larsen excused himself and left the room. In walked Ahmed Kureah, known as Abu Alaa, a senior PLO official in charge of the Financial Planning Department and Arafat's close confidant. He sat down in Larsen's seat according to plan and right on schedule.

Abu Alaa is a distinguished businessman, highly educated and a careful negotiator. We had met him briefly in Beirut in 1982 when he was the director of the highly successful SAMED, factories and workshops that were exporting Palestinian goods to several countries until the Israeli invasion of 1982 destroyed them. He had no record of involvement in the military (or "terrorist" in the Israeli lexicon) actions and was of sufficiently high rank to signal the seriousness of the PLO's commitment to the dialogue. The Israelis and the Palestinians knew that they had a match. It was agreed that they would report back to their respective leadership, maintain absolute secrecy, and begin substantive talks the following month . . . in Norway.

On January 20, 1993, the venue shifted to a mansion in the village of Sarpsborg, some sixty miles east of Oslo. The remote location, surrounded by wooded mountains, provided the psychological distance and relaxed atmosphere for secret meetings.

Abu Alaa arrived with two associates and Professor Hirschfeld with Professor Ron Pundak of Tel Aviv University. Staff at the mansion and those making travel arrangements were told that it was a meeting of academics who were working on a book. Prime Minister Holst would attend all of the fourteen sessions, facilitating direct negotiations as obstacles arose.

But more important, Holst and Larsen were sensitive to little cultural and interpersonal issues that might encourage a relaxed atmosphere, warm hospitality, and an increasing sense of trust. Relaxed meals that observed Jewish and Muslim dietary requirements, long informal conversations into the late hours of the evening, and many rounds of jokes are reported to have been among the confidence-building measures.

Tragic events in the Israeli-Palestinian theater repeatedly threatened to torpedo the negotiations. The occasional Israeli bombings of Lebanon; attacks on Israelis in south Lebanon and in the occupied territories by Lebanese or Palestinian militants; the Israeli curfew imposed on the territories and their reported use of "death squads" (Middle East Watch and B'Tselem), and the December 1992 expulsion of 415 Hamas supporters—all could have put an end to the negotiations. And, as recently as March 1993, several Israelis were killed in Israel and the Occupied Territories. The Israeli government responded by sealing off the territories, making travel from one district to the other impossible.

But the secret negotiations continued.

One of the major issues was deciding where to give Palestinians limited rights to rule themselves. During their February 1993 meetings, both parties agreed on the Gaza Strip. Growing popular opinion within the Labor party and the press had publicly called for a "Gaza First" option. However, the Palestinians could not accept Gaza alone, and they demanded Arab East Jerusalem, the heart of the occupied West Bank. The Israelis said no, and things appeared to be at an impasse.

Then in March, the negotiators finally settled on the poor, quiet but ancient city of Jericho, strategically important due to its access to the Jordan Valley and the Allenby Bridge (international crossing point between Israel and Jordan). Make no mistake, however, the Palestinians view this as a first step toward an eventual West Bank-Gaza Strip Palestinian state.

Until this time, Rabin and Peres had not been informed about the negotiations. Arafat was aware of them in general terms. Professor Hirschfeld contacted Deputy Foreign Minister Beilin, and they decided it was time to approach Shimon Peres.

By April, Peres and Arafat independently reviewed a draft of the agreement that had been written by Hirschfeld and Abu Alaa. Peres, who had been a bitter opponent of Rabin for two decades, decided it was time to approach the prime minister with the draft. Rabin was skeptical but cautiously gave the "green light." The PLO then insisted that it was time for meetings with Israeli officials within the Foreign Ministry, thereby equaling in political authority the commitment already made by the PLO.

The Israelis soon assigned Director general of the foreign ministry, Uri Savir, a brilliant young diplomat to the Norwegian channel. He was joined by Israeli expert in international law, Yoel Zinger, who had drafted the Israeli agreement to end the war in Lebanon (1982).

The Norwegians were perfect hosts. PLO and Israeli negotiators lived in the same houses or hotels as the venue shifted from one location to the other. They even spent several days in the home of Foreign Minister Holst where they ate sumptuous meals prepared by his wife. Mr. Larsen reported: "They shared a sense of humor as well. Each time tension rose, it was broken off by some joke, or by a cryptic reference to a joke they all understood. It was an informal relationship—intense, complex, characterized by passionate and silent poetry." (*New York Times*, September 5, 1993).

The Norwegian hosts disclosed a form of secret shorthand developed for confidentiality. Mr. Peres, Abu Alaa, and Holst were known as the "fathers," while Arafat and

Rabin were "the grandfathers." Officials at Beilin's and those under Abu Alaa were "the sons."

By June, both sides were prepared to move forward on the crucial issue of mutual (and simultaneous) recognition. The PLO had crossed that threshold in various Palestine National Council resolutions dating back to the mid-1970s, clarified in the November 1988 official recognition of Israel and the two-state solution. The Israelis had not come close to this position in an official fashion, as it was still illegal to even talk to the PLO. Now it appeared that mutual recognition could become a reality, but both sides decided to press the issue further.

The Israelis demanded that the PLO restate its recognition of Israeli in clear and uncertain terms, renounce terrorism, and reject several controversial sections of the PLO Covenant. The PLO, in turn, insisted on clear recognition of the PLO as the "sole legitimate representative of the Palestinian people." The PLO did not demand a similar renunciation of terrorism from Israel, causing concern among Arafat's critics. Nor did the PLO obtain a clear commitment from Israel on the vital issue of self-determination, leaving many Palestinians fearful that Arafat had abandoned hope of an independent Palestinian state.

These points proved to be among the most difficult even until three days prior to the September 13 ceremony. Israel refused to yield on "sole legitimate representative" language and preferred to call the PLO "representatives of the Palestinian people" (implying that there may be alternative "representatives" such as Jordan or Egypt). The language was changed, but even at the ceremony "PLO" was absent and needed to be inserted at the last minute in the text of the accord. The PLO claimed from its side that because it was a democracy, even Chairman Arafat and the Executive Committee did not have the authority to change the covenant, as it had been ratified by the Palestinian National Congress (the PNC). At this final stage the Norwegians involved not only Arafat and a trusted circle of advisors, but Rabin, Peres, and Egypt's Hosni Mubarak.

As late as Tuesday, September 7, the two sides were at an impasse. The PLO claimed that it had clearly renounced terrorism in 1988, and that no such demand was being placed on Israel. The Israelis insisted this pledge had been broken. Internal divisions within the PLO Executive Committee and shocking resignations from the Palestinian negotiating team added to the suspense and significantly raised the levels of anxiety.

Norway's Holst, Abu Alaa, and four Israeli negotiators, including Foreign Ministry Director General Uri Savir and legal counsel Yoel Singer, met secretly in the Hotel Bristol in Paris, on Tuesday, September 7, to save the plan. They labored frantically for nearly twenty-four hours to rescue two years of hard-won trust and the hope of peace. In addition to Abu Alaa, the PLO sent Yasser Abed Rabbo, one of the highest ranking members of the Executive Committee, and a high-level official of one of the two major Marxist parties in the PLO, the Democratic Front for the Liberation of Palestine (DFLP). In intense negotiations, involving a conference call to Arafat in Tunis, language was agreed upon by the Palestinians and Israel. Holst rushed to Charles DeGaulle Airport in Paris at 1:30 P.M. on Wednesday, hoping to secure Arafat's signature at his Tunis headquarters by early evening. At last, the most serious diplomatic impediment (to date) had been overcome.

Holst carried in his leather briefcase the following language that formed the basis for the diplomatic breakthrough:

The PLO recognizes the right of the State of Israel to exist in peace and security.

The PLO accepts United Nations Security Council Resolutions 242 and 338.

The PLO commits itself to the Middle East peace process, and to a peaceful resolution of the conflict between the two sides and declares that all outstanding issues relating to permanent status will be resolved through negotiations.

The PLO considers that the signing of the Declaration of Principles constitutes a historic event, inaugurating a new epoch of peaceful coexistence, free from violence and all other acts which endanger peace and stability.

Accordingly, the PLO renounces the use of terrorism and other acts of violence and will assume responsibility over all PLO elements and personnel in order to assure their compliance, prevent violations, and discipline violators. In view of the promise of a new era and the signing of the Declaration of Principles and based on Palestinian acceptance of Security Council Resolutions 242 and 338, the PLO affirms that those articles of the Palestinian Covenant which deny Israel's right to exist, and the provisions of the Covenant which are inconsistent with the commitments of this letter are now inoperative and no longer valid. Consequently, the PLO undertakes to submit to the Palestinian National Council for formal approval the necessary changes in regard to the Palestinian Covenant.

Sincerely, Yasser Arafat.

Although the date for the signing had been set for Monday, September 13, there was still sufficient confusion to leave both Palestinians and Israelis wondering if there might be a last-minute bombshell that would undermine the entire two years of careful diplomacy.

Day by day, as more news broke concerning the remarkable agreements, political opposition to both Arafat and Rabin charged the proposed peace initiative with emotion. Palestinian leaders, including high-ranking members of the Executive Committee, such as Foreign Minister Farouk Qaddoumi and Shafik al-Hout, denounced the accord as "a full-scale betrayal." Qaddoumi refused to represent the PLO in the Washington ceremony, and al-Hout resigned from the PNC. Al-Hout and others called for Arafat's immediate resignation and for Palestinians to reject the accord.

Highly respected Palestinian academic Dr. Riad Malki, professor at Birzeit University, and a leader of the Popular Front movement in the West Bank, stated: "We resisted the Israeli occupation and we will resist Palestinian autonomy." Reactions from more extreme elements such as Damascus-based Popular Front for the Liberation of Palestine (PFLP) General Command promised Arafat: "Your fate will be that of Anwar Sadat" (assassination). Hamas leaders in Amman burned Arafat's photo in public while their spokesman in the Gaza Strip said: "We will never agree to be part of this game."

On the Israeli side, hard-liners such as former Defense Minister and architect of the invasion of Lebanon Ariel Sharon claimed the accord will lead to a Palestinian State that will destroy Israel. Sharon rejected negotiations with the PLO and Arafat, whom he characterized as "a band of terrorists." Similar but slightly more articulate language came from Likud party leader Benjamin Netanyahu, who called for a national referendum on the deal that he characterized as "a launching pad for PLO attacks on Israel" (*TIME* magazine, September 13, 1993). Extremist Tsomet Party leader, Rafael Eitan, former Israeli Army Chief of Staff during the Lebanon invasion, charged the government with "signing an agreement with the greatest murderer of the Jews since Hitler" (Ibid.).

Despite the opposition, a corner had been turned. For most of the major parties now engaged in the process, there was no turning back. Certainly Arafat and his supporters within the PLO had achieved international recognition, pledges of desperately needed economic assistance, and a new process for negotiations to bypass the flawed Madrid process. For Rabin and the Labor party, the sense that they had achieved the best possible deal with a moderate Palestinian voice was a degree of assurance against the cries of the opposition.

For both, the decision was not as ideological as it was pragmatic. Quite simply, they realized that their respective citizens had only two choices: Learn to live together, or continue killing each other.

For too long they had chosen the latter.

3

Through Centuries of Conflict

Imagine waking up from a three-year coma and trying to understand the world in late 1993. The changes are almost beyond belief. First the Berlin Wall, then the Soviet Empire crumbles, followed by Nelson Mandela's release from prison and growing stature as a world leader negotiating directly with the white government of South Africa. Now this. The handshake still astonishes.

Now try to imagine this recent development in light of centuries of conflict in the region we call the Holy Land. In ancient times, Palestine was repeatedly conquered by invaders, including Egyptians, Assyrians, Babylonians, Alexander the Great, the Romans, and in 637 A.D., Muslims from Arabia, briefly the Crusaders from Europe in 1099, and in 1517, the Ottoman Turks.

The patriarch Abraham arrived in the Holy Land to find that the Canaanites welcomed him as he and Sarah sojourned and eventually settled among various Semitic peoples (Genesis 12–25). Melchizedek, a Canaanite "priest of God most high" (Genesis 14:18–20), brought bread and wine to Abraham and blessed him. The Scriptures later teach that God led the Hebrew tribes out of oppression under Moses' leadership, and after a circuitous route, to the Promised Land. Over the next 1200 years the independent nation Israel was short-lived under Saul, David, and Solomon. The Jewish Zealot revolt under the Maccabees in 163 B.C.E. brought another brief period of independence prior to Roman rule. The Romans crushed other rebellions in 66–70 C.E. and again in 131–34, expelling Jews from Palestine.

The Palestinians are a racially mixed people, descendants of the Canaanites, Philistines, and other Semitic tribes of Canaan. The population became largely Christian after the reign of Constantine, but most converted to Islam after the Arab conquest of 637 C.E. (What many people forget, however, is that an indigenous Christian community has lived in Palestine since Jesus' ministry and the day of Pentecost.)

The Crusades were a dark chapter for all the inhabitants of the Holy Land. The crusaders, who were essentially European Christian colonialists, killed Muslims, Jews, and Arab Christians side by side, memories of which remain centuries later for today's Palestinians (Amin Maahlouf, *The Crusades Through Arab Eyes*, Schocken Press, 1987).

Following the Crusaders' brief kingdoms, the Ottoman Turks captured Palestine early in the sixteenth century, holding it until World War I. Growing European anti-Semitism and persecution gave rise to modern Zionism, led by an Austrian Jewish journalist, Theodore Herzl. Herzl captured the sentiments of decades of European Jewish aspirations when he wrote *Der Judenstad* (*The Jewish State*, published in 1896) and convened the first Zionist Congress in Basel, Switzerland. The rallying cry was: "A land without people for a people without land." But Palestine was fully inhabited by approximately 600,000 people when Herzl wrote these words, with 94 percent being Palestinian Muslims and Christians, and less than 7 percent Jews. The British census of 1922 showed a population of 757,182, of whom 83,794 were Jews (10 percent).

As Ottoman Turkish rule crumbled and the Allied Powers defeated them in World War I, the British received the Mandate for Palestine. But before the war had been completed, the British had promised the Arabs independence if they would join their war effort against the Turks, a campaign glorified in the Lawrence of Arabia story. The secret McMahon Correspondence of 1916 promised Amir Hussein, sharif of Mecca, independence for all the Arabs should they fight with the British. However, the British and French concluded a secret treaty, the Sykes-Picot Agreement, that called for the Eastern Mediterranean to be divided between them. Their formula prevailed in the treaties that settled World War I. However, the mutually exclusive promises by the British were impossible to satisfy.

The other vital part of the Allied post-war plan was the promise made to the Zionists by the British in what is known as the Balfour declaration of November 1917. The Declaration stated in part that the British viewed with favor the creation of a "homeland for the Jews"—but it should not impinge upon the cultural and religious rights of the Arab population. The latter clause was essentially ignored as British policy supported accelerated settlement of Jews in Palestine and the basic provisions for an eventual Jewish state. Various official British and American commissions recommended that Palestine be either a binational democracy or that two separate states be created.

Jewish and Arab relations in Palestine deteriorated considerably during the 1930s and 1940s as rebellion and various expressions of opposition broke out. A major Palestinian revolt in 1936 was brutally crushed by the British with assistance from Jewish militia they had trained. But far more serious was the impact of the horrible Jewish persecution and genocide perpetrated by the Nazis in Europe. Increased Jewish immigration during these years was directed toward Palestine as many Western governments limited the number of Jewish refugees they would accept. "We became the victims of the victims of the Nazis," says Fr. Elias Chacour, a pacifist and Palestinian priest whose family was expelled from Galilee.

After World War II, the British decided to leave Palestine, turning the turbulent situation over to the newly established United Nations. On November 29, 1947, the General Assembly of the UN voted to partition Palestine into independent Arab and Jewish states. The Jewish state would include more than 50 percent of the territory of Palestine, and it would receive major Palestinian population centers and the richest coastal land. This despite the fact that Jews made up only one-third of the population in 1947. The Arabs rejected the plan, and the Arab states declared war.

One of the most historic events of modern Middle East history came when Israel declared itself a state on May 14, 1948. The following day, Arab armies attacked Israel, but the more heavily armed Israeli forces prevailed, extending their control to 78 percent of Palestine, more than it would have received under the United Nations plan. The war resulted in a massive forced expulsion of the Palestinian population, with approximately 760,000 becoming refugees. Palestinians still call it *Al Nakhbah*, the disaster. Thus began the Palestinian refugee crisis, which remains unsettled today.

Recognizing that they must take their destiny into their own hands and desiring to keep their sense of national aspirations alive, the increasingly frustrated Palestinians formed the Palestine Liberation Organization under the sponsorship of the Arab League in 1964. Some feel the move was originally intended by the Arab nations to control the Palestinians. Yasser Arafat was elected chairman of the PLO (see chapter 4—"Yasser Arafat and the PLO").

In 1967, however, one of the most pivotal events in

modern Middle East history took place: the Six Day War. In June, Israeli forces scored a lightning victory over their Arab neighbors, capturing Syria's Golan Heights, Jordan's West Bank and Arab East Jerusalem, and Egypt's Sinai Desert and the Gaza Strip. Thus began a new, expanded Israeli military occupation of Arab land and a new stage of the Arab confrontations with Israel.

These confrontations escalated until October 1973, when Egypt and Syria launched a surprise attack on Israel. Israel suffered a crippling blow, while Arab armies performed admirably in their own view. Also, the Arab oil-producing states initiated the now-famous oil embargo of late 1973–74, throwing panic into the world marketplace and creating long lines of vehicles at gasoline pumps in the West.

In 1974, a majority of Arab states formally recognized the PLO as the "sole legitimate representative of the Palestinian people." Arafat addressed the UN General Assembly and the UN gave the PLO observer status. That was too much for security-conscious Israel. As the PLO built a social and military infrastructure in southern Beirut and the south coastal portion of Lebanon, some Lebanese political-military groups and Israel began to plot against the Palestinians. During this period there were constant raids by Israel on the PLO in Lebanon, and by the PLO on Israel. In March 1978, Israel invaded southern Lebanon, only partially withdrawing two months later but retaining a security strip above the Israeli border that remains today.

In June 1982, after an eleven-month cease fire, Israel again invaded Lebanon in a massive air, land, and sea assault. The outcome of the three-month war was inconclusive, but it *did* disperse the PLO into eight Arab countries, with Yasser Arafat establishing new headquarters in Tunis. Eventually, Israel became bogged down in a costly military occupation of Lebanon, vulnerable to guerrilla attacks and psychological terror. Back home, more than four hundred thousand Israelis marched in the streets against their government's involvement in Lebanon and their role in the massacre at Sabra and Shatilla.

In December 1987, a spontaneous uprising began first in the poverty-stricken Jabaliyeh refugee camp on the Gaza Strip and spread quickly throughout the occupied territories. The uprising was soon called the *Intifada* or, correctly translated, "the shaking off" (of occupation and oppression). The impact of Palestinian youth facing the Israeli army with stones and being felled by bullets stunned the world. At the same time, leaders of the *Intifada* pushed the PLO leadership to adopt a clear two-state solution and negotiate directly with its enemy, Israel. On November 15, 1988, the Palestine National Council took this decision and declared that the Palestinian state would live beside Israel in peace. Arafat stated the PLO's acceptance of Israel, renunciation of violence, and willingness to negotiate a peaceful settlement based on United Nations resolutions.

Meanwhile, phenomenal events on the world stage seemed destined to affect, either positively or negatively, the Palestinian situation. The collapse of the Soviet Union left only the United States to wield influence across the Middle East. After Saddam Hussein invaded and occupied Kuwait, the United States exercised its power by rallying most of the United Nations to defeat Iraq. During the Gulf War there was also renewed speculation among Western evangelical Christians concerning the prophetic meaning of the latest Middle East conflict, with some pointing to Iraq as the revived Babylonian Empire and the rise of the Antichrist through the United Nations. As in the past, the role of Israel was pivotal in these interpretations, leading many to view the war as another sign that we were in the latter days, counting down to Armageddon.

After careful strategic work by U.S. Secretary of State James Baker, including warnings to Israeli's Likud government to cease new settlements in Jerusalem and the West Bank, the Madrid Peace Negotiations opened in November 1991. Baker's efforts brought great promise and credibility, but his eventual withdrawal to oversee President Bush's faltering campaign in late 1992 put the negotiations on the back burner. The Shamir-led Likud government, always a reluctant partner, tied up the Madrid negotiations (some say, intentionally) with a series of conditions that frustrated both sides. After twenty-two months of absolute frustration, the Palestinian negotiators threatened to boycott the tenth round, scheduled for Washington, D.C., in early September 1993.

Not knowing about the secret Norwegian channel or the recently concluded security discussions between Israel and the PLO, negotiators on the Palestinian side threatened to return to their constituents in the West Bank and Gaza Strip who were increasingly opposed to negotiations. Arafat and those top PLO executives who were aware that the secret channels were close to bearing fruit prevailed upon the Palestinian negotiators to return for one more round. Just as they were about to return, the news began to leak out first to the Israeli press, and then to the international press, of the phenomenal breakthrough.

For the first time in nearly one hundred years of conflict, it looked as though Israel and the PLO would at least make a commitment toward peace.

The supremacy of military victory eluded both Israelis and Palestinians for a generation. The Palestinian suffering

in Lebanon and occupied Palestinian territories, combined
with innocent Jewish blood shed throughout these years,
propels us to rejoice in this small, initial step toward peace.
But will it bring peace?

We will attempt to answer that in the part 2, but for now,
I will close this chapter with a story that was circulating in
Lebanon after the 1982 Israeli invasion.

It seems that God called together Menachem Begin,
Ronald Reagan, and Yasser Arafat after the tragic Lebanon
War of 1982. God gave each one wish. Begin asked:
"Yahweh, will Israel be secure and have a long life?" God
smiled and said, "Yes, but not for fifty years." Begin cried
because he would not see it in his lifetime. Then Reagan
asked: "Will the United States triumph over the Soviet
Union and defeat godless communism?" "Yes," said God,
but not for ten years. Reagan cried because he might not see
it in his lifetime.

Then the diminutive Arafat strolled up with his freshly
pressed uniform and *keffiyeh* and asked: "Allah, will the
Palestinians have their own independent state with dignity
and full rights?" Then God cried.

Perhaps the hopelessness reflected in this story will
begin to turn around for both peoples and within our
lifetime bring security, dignity, justice, and peace to the
Christians, Jews, and Muslims who consider this region holy.

(Two excellent sources on the Holy Land are Harold
Wilson, *The Chariot of Israel*, W. W. Norton, London, 1981;
Colin Chapman, *Whose Promised Land?* Lion Publishing,
1983.)

4

Arafat and the PLO

Yasser Araft is, without doubt, the most intriguing personality in the Middle East. Not only has he survived dozens of assassination attempts and a near-fatal plane crash from which he has emerged with a near-legendary status as a survivor, he has weathered many cycles of Middle East political upheaval. With his distinctive stubble, military fatigues, and *keffiyeh* draped carefully over his head and shoulders in the very shape of Palestine, he has become the enduring symbol of the Palestinian struggle for liberation and statehood.

Arafat was born Rahman Abdul Rauf Arafat-al-Qudwa al-Husseini in 1929 and picked up the nickname "Yasser" as a boy. He came from a family of seven children and a financially comfortable home. He grew up in Egypt and became active in the Palestinian cause while studying engineering at Cairo University. He was a classmate and lifelong friend of Pope Shenouda, patriarch of the Coptic Orthodox church. After working for two years in Egypt, he moved to Kuwait, where he lived for about eight years. He built a contracting business with partners and was well on his way to becoming a millionaire.

Of his childhood, Arafat says little except to acknowledge that he was born in Gaza and lost his mother when he was four years old. He grew up in the old city of Jerusalem

with an uncle before moving to be with his father in Cairo
and begin courses in civil engineering.

Abandoning the good life for the Palestinian cause, he
helped to found Al Fatah in 1956 and became chairman of
the PLO in 1969. He has always considered himself a
freedom fighter, not a terrorist as many claim. He eagerly
points out that George Washington was called a terrorist by
the British; likewise, DeGaulle by the Nazis; and the
Algerians by the French. He also reminds us that in his early
years, Menacham Begin was considered a terrorist, implying
that whenever one fights "underground" against an occupy-
ing army, he is a terrorist to the army but a hero to those
being oppressed.

Both Dan and I have met Arafat and consider him a
charismatic leader who is solely devoted to establishing a
state for the people called Palestinians. Despite his militaris-
tic image, he has gone on record as accepting the possibility
of a Palestinian state that would not have an army. And once
you get past the grizzled look and trademark sidearm, it is
easy to see why he is so popular among his followers. He is
animated, passionate about his cause but also has a sense of
humor and enjoys a good story. A skilled politician, Arafat
recognized me at the White House ceremony and greeted
me warmly.

Many feel that by signing the accord, Arafat has signed
his own death warrant. In typical Arab fashion, however,
Arafat accepts his fate as being in the hands of Allah. Those
close to the late Egyptian president, Anwar Sadat, say he also
believed his role in the Camp David Accord would be
rewarded by the assassin's bullet. Whatever you think of
Arafat, you cannot deny the fact that his secret negotiations
and eventual signing of an accord with Israel is a courageous
act that could cost him his life.

Arafat's position as Chairman of the PLO is tantamount

to being the president or chief executive of a nation. For despite the controversy stirred by those three letters— PLO—it forms the basic structure for a government in exile. If the Palestinians indeed get their homeland, they will have the advantage of a governing structure already in place.

The Palestine Liberation Organization was founded in 1964 by the Arab League in part to control the Palestinians. Because of Arafat's total dedication to the cause and unsullied reputation, he was asked by the majority of his colleagues to become the chairman of the PLO in 1969.

The PLO is an umbrella organization with labor movements, hospitals, educational institutions, administration and finance, social welfare, and military forces under its purview. The PLO is answerable to the Palestine National Council, a parliamentary body currently based in Amman, Jordan.

Israel's deep-seated fear of the PLO has *some* justification, based, in part, on the original PLO charter, which rejected Zionism and called for a secular democratic state. Despite assurances that this part of the charter was no longer operative, it has always stood in the way of serious negotiations between Israel and the PLO. Why bargain with a group that is founded on the belief that we should not exist? reasoned Israeli leaders. With the peace accord's provision for that section of the charter to be renounced, Israel became more open to a negotiated settlement.

Few people of our generation thought we would see the day when an Israeli prime minister would shake hands with *any* representative of the PLO. But it happened and it at least deserves our respect. Yitzhak Rabin and Yasser Arafat demonstrated tremendous courage on that sunny September afternoon, but what happens next is literally anyone's guess.

Part II

What Could
Still Happen
in the Holy Land?

by Dan O'Neill

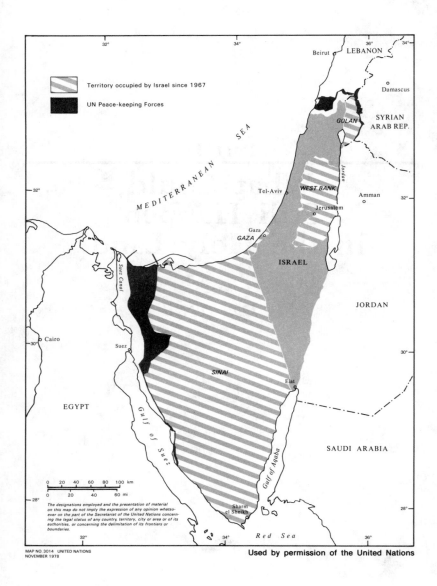

Territory occupied by Israel since 1967

UN Peace-keeping Forces

MAP NO. 3014 UNITED NATIONS
NOVEMBER 1978

The designations employed and the presentation of material
on this map do not imply the expression of any opinion whatsoever on the part of the Secretariat of the United Nations concerning the legal status of any country, territory, city or area or of its
authorities, or concerning the delimitation of its frontiers or
boundaries.

5

Peace Agreement
or Death Warrant?

From the moment that Arafat and Rabin shook hands, one question seemed to loom before everyone: Now what? Will this really bring peace to this violent region, or will it signal yet a new era of attacks and reprisals? In many quarters pessimism prevails, for despite the immense trust represented by the two men who signed the agreement, *dis*trust seems to reign.

A Palestinian human-rights worker captured the feelings of many of her people and of Israelis as well: "I feel like the Red Sea has just parted and we don't know what to do next. We are elated that we might be free from the occupation, but we cannot fully trust that it is the case. Is this real freedom or a mirage? Will this lead eventually to our self-determination and future state? Are the Palestinian leaders just being set up by a clever American and Israeli trick? This may become another form of occupation under another name. It could even lead to an Armageddon-like bloodbath if it does not lead to real peace."

For Amos Oz, Israel's greatest living writer and a leader of the Israeli peace movement, the September 13, 1993, signing of the Middle East Accord was the second most important event in the history of modern Israel. Oz told BBC radio, "Only one moment in history equals this for me—the creation of the Jewish state by the United Nations resolution in 1947. And that also was achieved by compromise."

But the leader of the rightist Likud party in Israel, former Israeli representative to the United Nations, Benjamin Netanyahu, reflected the views of those in the powerful settler movement, the military, and Likud supporters when he wrote an op-ed piece in the *New York Times*:

> The plan effectively establishes P.L.O. control over all the territory up to the pre-1967 border—ten miles from Tel Aviv and two miles from downtown Jerusalem. . . . What will happen when terrorists attack Israelis in Jerusalem and return to nearby P.L.O. land? Or fire rockets from hills above Tel Aviv? The Israeli Army will have no right to enter the territory and root them out. This, believe it or not, is the "internal" responsibility of Yasir Arafat (*New York Times*, September 12, 1993).

According to a public-opinion poll conducted by the largest circulation newspaper in Israel, *Yediot Ahronot*, during the week before the signing ceremony the accord had a narrow margin of support among Israelis (53 percent supported it, while 45 percent opposed it). Two days after the ceremony the support jumped to 67 percent.

A similar spectrum of opinion could be found on the Palestinian side. Dr. George Habash, leader of the Marxist-oriented Popular Front for the Liberation of Palestine, reflected the feelings of many Palestinians in the diaspora and under occupation, when he told Monte Carlo Radio on August 30 that the proposed deal was "a trick to rob Palestinians of their legitimate rights."

Leaders of the Islamic movement Hamas have gone even further in their verbal rejection of the accord, but as of

October 1, 1993, there is an uneasy truce between Hamas and Arafat's mainstream Fatah party.

Even the leading Palestinian intellectual living in the United States, Dr. Edward Said of Columbia University, said:

> The deal before us smacks of the P.L.O. leadership's exhaustion and isolation and of Israel's shrewdness. Many Palestinians are asking themselves why, after years of concessions, we should be conceding once again to Israel and the United States in return for promises and vague improvements in the occupation that won't all occur until the "final status" talks some three to five years hence, and perhaps not even then (The *Nation,* September 20, 1993).

Dr. Sari Nusseibeh, a Palestinian intellectual from Jerusalem with a Ph.D. from Cambridge and former professor of philosophy at Birzeit University, reflected the views of the majority when he told the *New York Times* after the ceremony:

> We hope this is a turning point. It opens up a lot of potential for this area and for the two people. But it is a very fragile agreement, fraught with explosives, and one has to nurture it very tenderly to make sure that it grows—on both sides (*New York Times,* September 14, 1993).

The truth is, nobody can predict what will happen. Will this peace process continue in the face of all these doubts? Will the polarization within both the Jewish and Palestinian communities lead to civil wars in each of their societies? A closer look at the contents and promises of the accord itself will help answer those critical questions.

Goal of the Agreement

The stated aim of the agreement is to create an interim Palestinian self-government that will be run by an elected council to serve for a maximum of five years while negotiations move toward a final settlement. Let us be absolutely clear that the accord is not a peace treaty but is an interim agreement. The agreement is divided into seventeen articles that cover a variety of formulas for relationships between the government of Israel and the interim Palestinian authority.

Elections

The agreement calls for "direct, free, and general political elections" under international observation for membership in the Council. The intent is to allow the Palestinian people in the West Bank and Gaza Strip to "govern themselves according to democratic principles." The Council will have the power to pass laws that will be applicable only to the areas within its jurisdiction. The elections will be held in June 1994. Jerusalem will not be included in the area the Council will control, but Palestinian residents of Arab East Jerusalem will vote in the elections.

Limited Palestinian Authority

The elected Palestinian Council will have jurisdiction over only the Palestinian population in the Gaza Strip and Jericho. It will not have authority over approximately 45 percent of the Gaza Strip, which is occupied by nearly four thousand Jewish settlers and the military. The Council will be granted authority over such local matters as education, culture, health, social welfare, the environment, direct taxation, and tourism. The authority will not include external security, the Jewish settlements, and international relations.

Israeli Pullback

The announced Israeli pullback begins on December 13, 1993, from the areas populated by Palestinians in the Gaza Strip and Jericho, with troops remaining in the settlements and military sectors. The document calls for a "smooth and peaceful transfer of authority" from the Israeli Defense Forces to the new Palestinian authority. The document also calls for the "redeployment" of the Israeli military in the remainder of the West Bank, but "outside the populated areas." Israeli settlers, other citizens of Israel, and the military will have free access to all roads. On September 28, 1993, Israel announced that it will abide by the pullback date and that Yasser Arafat will be allowed to establish headquarters in Jericho on January 1, 1994.

Security

The Palestinian police force will assume responsibility for maintaining "internal security and public order" in the Palestinian population sectors of the Gaza Strip and Jericho, while the Israeli Defense Forces (IDF) will maintain security within the settlements and military zones. The precise relationships between the IDF and Palestinian police on more complex issues are yet to be determined. However, disputes between Palestinians and Israelis are to be referred to a joint committee, and be subject to arbitration if both sides disagree.

Jewish Settlements

The status and future of the Israeli settlements in the West Bank and Gaza Strip will continue to be a major issue of dispute. The Israeli Defense Forces will provide protection for Israeli settlers living in the West Bank and Gaza Strip, but the agreement is vague on the extent of that protection, and the authority of the IDF, particularly when settlers engage in various activities within the Palestinian areas.

Economic Cooperation

An Israeli-Palestinian economic-cooperation committee will be established to develop modes of cooperation in managing water resources in the West Bank and Gaza Strip; in producing and maintaining electricity resources; in creating a cooperative energy development program that will provide for oil and gas exploration and use; cooperation in the field of finance, including a joint financial development and action program for investment in the West Bank and Gaza Strip, and a Palestinian development bank; in the field of international trade, with the hope of creating free-trade zones in the Gaza Strip and Israel; creating a joint Israeli-Palestinian industrial research and development center; and both a human resources development plan and an environmental protection plan.

Refugees

A special committee will be established to decide on the possible repatriation of one-hundred thousand to two-hundred thousand Palestinian refugees displaced from the West Bank and Gaza Strip in 1967. However, the agreement delays negotiations on the 700,000-760,000 refugees displaced during 1948 and in subsequent years, whose descendants today number upward of three million. Thus, half of the Palestinians in the world have yet to see their status resolved.

Jerusalem

One of the most complicated political and emotional issues is the future status of Jerusalem, which the agreement postpones until final negotiations. Jerusalem is the spiritual and political heart and head of both the Jewish Israeli and Palestinian Christian and Muslim populations. Each side views Jerusalem as the future capital of their state. The status of the city, the holy places, access to the religious sites, protection of the populations, and other vital questions during a prolonged interim period will undoubtedly be a major bone of contention.

Human Rights

Many aspects of the agreement, particularly the transfer of power and authority, have raised significant concerns from international human-rights organizations and local Israeli and Palestinian human-rights agencies. The New York-based organization Middle East Watch, a division of the global international Human Rights Watch, issued a memorandum to the government of Israel and the Palestine Liberation Organization "to make human rights a top priority." Identical letters were handed to Prime Minister Rabin and Chairman Arafat to underscore Middle East Watch's concern for the safety of both populations. Middle East Watch rightly noted that "future progress in resolving the conflict may depend on initiatives taken now toward curbing violations of human rights."

Among the many serious concerns is the ongoing debate between Israel and the United Nations and international human-rights organizations, over the application of the Fourth Geneva Conventions (1949) to the West Bank, East Jerusalem, and Gaza Strip. According to international law and previous United Nations resolutions, the Conventions are applicable to the Palestinian civilian population in these areas, but Israel has refused to recognize and implement this standard. Both the mechanisms for enforcement and the agreement with the government of Israel must be implemented during the interim period lest the entire peace process be jeopardized. To underscore these concerns, the first official committee that the PLO requested to establish when Arafat and Rabin met in Cairo on October 5, 1993, was a high-level commission on human rights.

But the chair of the Israeli League for Human and Civil Rights, a Holocaust survivor and professor emeritus at Hebrew University, Dr. Israel Shahak, expressed his concerns over the human-rights situation, which he fears may worsen in the coming years:

> The Agreement means that Arafat is now annexed by the American-Israeli security system. In return he will get nothing except permission to be a local dictator. The human rights situation may even qualitatively deteriorate (The *Nation*, "Minority Report," October 11, 1993).

Human-rights organizations, nongovernmental organizations (affiliated with the United Nations), churches, and others will have a major role to play in the human-rights field throughout the coming years.

Still, the underlying theme here is hope, guarded hope, that this new opening might offer. Both Israelis and Palestinians have a hunger for and a proven record on democracy. A successful Palestinian democratization process during the next three years will be a beacon of hope in the Middle East. But the enforcement of internationally recognized human-rights norms will be the litmus test of the heralded democracy of both peoples.

Another source of hope is the high education rate and degree of professional training of both peoples. Everyone is aware of Israel's technical capabilities in the fields of agriculture, electronics, and military sophistocation. Palestinians have the highest educational rate in the entire Arab world and a higher Ph.D. rate per capita than the Israeli population. Israeli Jews and Palestinian Arabs have vast reservoirs of highly trained professionals, accumulated over four decades. The two peoples, when given the chance with internationally enforced provisions for human rights and security, could develop an economic miracle in the Holy Land.

The major responsibility to enable the peace agreement to be successful lies with the international community, especially the United States and other member nations of the United Nations, and then with Israel and the Palestinian people themselves. The international community must ensure that the June 1994 elections are supervised, strictly fair and peaceful, conducted according to democratic procedures, have no Israeli or other Arab nation interference, and that the results are fully implemented. The vast network of nongovernmental organizations, human rights and peace organizations, churches, synagogues, mosques, and major interfaith organizations can play a significant role in urging their governments to remain accountable for justice and peace.

So while the accord does not guarantee peace, it does provide a framework for working through the several difficult issues that threaten peaceful relations between Israel and the PLO. Anthony Lewis of the *New York Times* captured the hopes of many:

> The risks are great. The opponents on both sides are armed and angry. But I do not think the ultras will win the political argument. Peace has too great a momentum when it becomes a reality for the grasping. Israelis are tired of sending their sons to the West Bank to keep down another people. Most Palestinians, too, want a chance to live a normal life (*New York Times*).

6

Barriers to Peace
in the Holy Land

*From the least to the greatest, all are greedy for gain; prophets
and priests alike, all practice deceit. They dress the wound of
my people as though it were not serious. "Peace, peace," they
say, when there is no peace.*

JEREMIAH 8:10–11

A*s former State Department official* William Quandt recently
noted, events like the dramatic September 13 Middle East
Peace Accord sometimes take on a creative energy of their
own. He cites Richard Nixon's trip to China, the fall of the
Berlin Wall, and the release of Nelson Mandela from prison,
as examples.

"What these historical moments have in common,"
Quandt writes, "is that they suddenly change the way we
look at problems that were seemingly intractable. . . . Sights
are raised, minds briefly opened, hopes allowed to soar"
(*Washington Post*, September 12, 1993).

But will sights continue to be raised when an Israeli
settler is shot to death or a Palestinian murdered? The peace
is fragile, and hope could evaporate quickly in the months
and years leading up to the "final phase" of December 1998.
The dark and bloody scenes of Beirut and the genocide in

the former Yugoslavia loom as ever-present possibilities for the Israeli and Palestinian people.

One major threat to the hoped-for peace is extremism—rejectionists among the Israelis, Arabs in general, and the Palestinians themselves. Here are some potential barriers to the peace accord:

Israeli Rejectionists

Among the hard-liners currently active are such well-known figures as Ariel Sharon, a member of the Knesset, former defense minister, and architect of the invasion of Lebanon. Another Knesset member is former military chief of staff Rafael Eitan who heads a militant pro-settler party, Tsomet. Several others hold extremist views. They see all of the West Bank and Gaza Strip as Israeli territory, Eretz Yisrael ("Greater Israel"). Fierce opponents of the Labor party are keen on regaining political power, they are capable of stirring the passions of hatred that can lead to armed attacks on the Palestinian population.

Among the most extreme are leaders of the Gush Emunim settler movement that has in the recent past included terrorist cells (See Ian Lustick, *For the Land and the Lord*, New York: Council on Foreign Relations Press, 1988). Many are driven by a religious ideology that believes God gave the Holy Land to Jews alone, and they are called to exterminate modern descendants of the Amalekites. Other settlers are driven by a more pragmatic political ideology of Jewish control of Eretz Yisrael and maintain that the sworn enemies of the Jews are the PLO, Islam, and the Arab nations.

In the late-1970 to early-1980 period, a settler terrorist network was uncovered that had been responsible for the assassination of Palestinian mayors in the West bank, armed attacks on university students, and sniper activity on Palestinian civilians in the West Bank. Israeli political analysts believe these cells have been reorganized and exist today in the West Bank and Israel. Having been trained as Israeli military personnel and knowledgeable in the fields of guerrilla warfare and highly sophistocated explosives, they could wreak havoc in the Palestinian population centers and assassinate key Palestinian leaders.

After the agreement was announced to Israelis, the settlement movement and Likud began to organize opposition. Angry settlers began to demonstrate outside of the prime minister's office on a daily basis, calling Rabin a "traitor." A group of orthodox rabbis warned Rabin that "a civil war is likely to break out as a result of (the government's) dangerous and crazy steps" (*Newsweek,* September 3, 1993). One is reminded of the battle that settlers had with the Israeli army following the Camp David Accord when they needed to be forcibly removed. The West Bank is a far more emotional and religious reality for the settlers, and Israeli withdrawal from key areas in the future may become bloody.

Palestinian Rejectionists

Rejectionists among the Palestinians include the anti-PLO group Abu-Nidal, recognized as one of the most dangerous international terrorist operations in the world. The Abu-Nidal group has attempted to assassinate Yasser Arafat on numerous occasions and has killed a number of Palestinian peace leaders.

The Popular Front for the Liberation of Palestine-General Command (PFLP-GC), based in Damascus and led by Ahmad Jabril, has been responsible for a variety of terrorist incidents and accused of others, such as the Pan-Am Lockerbie tragedy. PFLP-GC is believed to have in its possession the most sophisticated plasticine explosives available. They have called for the death of Arafat as a traitor to the Palestinian cause.

Then there is a cluster of Lebanese, Sudanese, Egyptians, Jordanians, and Palestinians who want to see Khoumeini-style Islamic states established throughout the Middle East. These fiercely anti-Western movements have gained significant followings in Lebanon, where the Hezbollah ("Party of God") movement has been resisting Israeli occupation of southern Lebanon for a decade. On September 13, as the accord was signed, a major Hezbollah demonstration called for "Death to Arafat." Six demonstrators were shot to death by the Lebanese army.

U.S. State Department analysis believes that the network of pro-Iranian militants are underwritten by Iran, with training and funding passing through Sudan, and now threatening Egypt. Ironically, the movement has recruited many of the Mujahadeen who where trained by the United States in Afghanistan and Pakistan to fight the Soviet army. The Sheikh Omar Abdel-Rahman group, accused of the bombing of the New York City Trade Towers, are believed to be affiliated with the Iranian-Sudanese network.

Independent of these networks but clearly influenced by their Islamic theology and political program is the Hamas movement, now growing rapidly in the West Bank and Gaza Strip. In addition to Hamas is the Islamic Jihad movement. Both groups are capable of rallying major military actions against the Israeli army and settlements, and possibly against the PLO mainstream.

Many of the Hamas leaders are serious scholars, professionals, and religious leaders. Highly respected in their communities, especially the Gaza Strip, their popularity skyrocketed among Palestinians when Israel expelled 415 Hamas leaders in December 1992. Evangelical leaders Len Rodgers of Venture Middle East and Brother Andrews of

Open Doors visited the expelees in January 1993, extending their compassion, but they were denounced by some Christian fundamentalists closely aligned with the state of Israel. The Hamas leaders must be included in all future negotiations and have the option of fielding their own candidates in elections, or they are capable of sabotaging the peace process.

As of this writing in early October 1993, Arafat's mainstream Fatah movement has reached an uneasy truce with Hamas, whereby Hamas will not embark on actions that will undermine the accord, while it reserves the right to oppose the agreement.

The bottom line for most of the rejectionist factions on both sides of the issue is their unwillingness to consider a compromise on certain major issues and their particular dogmas. From Ariel Sharon and many settlers who view the PLO and Arafat as Nazis and Adolf Hitler bent on killing Jews, to Ahmad Jabril who views Arafat as a collaborator with the West and a corrupt traitor needing to be assassinated, clearly each side in the conflict have their "shadowy wild cards" and are capable of jeopardizing this fragile peace process. But the rejectionists should not be confused with those critics of the accord who have sincere grievances.

Opponents Within the PLO

Coming from the opposite political spectrum from Hamas but opposing the accord with equal fervor, are the two major Marxist parties of the PLO, the Popular Front for the Liberation of Palestine (PLFP), led by Dr. George Habash, and the Democratic Front (DFLP), led by Nayef Hawatmeh. Both of these leaders are Palestinian Christians, and their movements have had significant respect and support from Palestinian academics and professionals, as well as at the grass roots. These are serious, highly intellectual, and devoted people who believe that the present accord is an Israeli "trick" designed to set up the PLO for eventual defeat and give Israel permanent control of the West Bank under the guise of peace.

Ali Jeddah, a Palestinian journalist from the Old City of Jerusalem, reflects the sincere anguish and bitterness of many Palestinians who support the PFLP and DFLP. Jeddah, who spent seventeen years in Israeli prisons, said:

> We are not heading toward a stable peace. It is a total subjection of the Palestinians to Israeli and American conditions. They are not talking about self-determination, establishing an independent state with Jerusalem as its capital, and there's no mention of the right of return. . . . I want peace, but real peace between equals. This is artificial, and it won't last long (*New York Times*, September 14, 1993).

Ali Jeddah is a sincere, serious, and representative Palestinian whose words speak for hundreds of thousands of Palestinians, both inside the occupied territories and in the diaspora. The concerns he raises must be taken with the utmost seriousness by the world but most especially by the Israeli and PLO leadership who will negotiate during the next five years.

The potential for this peace agreement to hold together for the critical 1993–95 period will depend on whether Israeli fears over security can be reduced and whether Palestinians will experience rapid, specific, and real change in their economic condition and political status. Unlike the Norwegian-brokered, secret peace negotiations that were hidden from the world to protect the process and the negotiators, everything will be out in the open and under an international magnifying glass. Each incident of political terrorism, every human-rights violation, inevitable delays by the Israeli army or Palestinian civil authority to implement change on schedule will be known by the world. But like the Norwegian process, there may be the potential for slowly creating an atmosphere for coexistence and confidence building.

So what the accord really offers is an opportunity and a challenge. The process will need patience, economic support, and mutual accountability. And from people of faith, it will need prayer.

7

Best- and Worst-Case Scenarios

One of the great traditions of Middle East culture is the gathering of men (and, recently, women) in a coffee shop or hotel lobby to discuss politics and speculate on future events. No doubt, those venues are active in Jewish and Arab communities as men and women try to guess how events will unfold in the next weeks and months. In that spirit, then, we offer four scenarios, any of which could play itself out on the Middle East stage.

Islamic Supremacy

The worst case for the Israelis might be the assassination of Yasser Arafat (which many consider a *real* possibility), followed by the collapse of the PLO and its replacement by Hamas, a movement committed to establishing an Islamic state between the Mediterranean and Jordan River. If the Hamas leaders look toward Iran and Hezbollah in Lebanon for their political models, Israel will have much to fear. Such an Islamic state will allow only limited rights granted to Jews and Christians, and Islamic law will be implemented. If the Hamas movement is excluded by the PLO leadership, significant internal tension will escalate into violence. Also, some Hamas leaders are not opposed to employing military measures against Israel now. Guerrilla operations against

Israeli settlers, the military, and others would become common. If the Islamic movements are successful in Egypt, Jordan, and Lebanon, Israel would then be surrounded by militant Iranian-styled Islamic governments. The present fears of Ariel Sharon and Benjamin Netanyahu could be realized: the gradual annihilation of the Jewish state. These developments are highly unlikely, yet they will be articulated continually by various elements within the Israeli body politic as well as by their adherents in the West.

Militant Jewish Opposition

On the Palestinian side, a worst-case scenario would involve the breakdown of all civil rule and human rights in the occupied territories (including the new Palestinian Gaza Strip and Jericho) leading to internecine Palestinian violence, even a civil war as occurred in Lebanon following the 1982 invasion by Israel. After the Lebanon War, Israel withdrew its forces from certain areas, allowing extremist militias to enter refugee camps still under Israeli military control. As seen by some Arabs, the massacre of Palestinians at Sabra and Shatila was blamed on Arafat for not negotiating for their security but instead, trusting American and Israeli promises. The PLO then splintered as a former military leader close to Arafat, Abu Musa, joined Ahmed Jabril's PFLP-General Command (and others) to attack Arafat and Fatah in a series of ferocious battles. Significant blood was shed before Arafat fled from Tripoli in the north of Lebanon.

It is entirely possible that extremist settlers and other forces within Israel will attempt similar massacres that could lead to chaos in the Gaza Strip, or in the occupied West Bank. At that point we can be certain that Israeli Defense Forces will attack quickly and massively. Current Israeli deputy chief of staff for the IDF, Amnon Shahak, stated as much, noting that the Israeli army will remain responsible for "the overall security of Israelis" and for "defending against internal threats." Deputy Defense Minister Morde-chai Gur added: "During the negotiations we will redeter-mine the conditions, means, and methods that will allow the IDF to reach any corner to make sure that we can carry out our responsibility for the safety of all Israelis" (*New York Times,* Sept. 3, 1993).

In other words, if Hamas and the PLO, or any combina-tion of Palestinian armies began a civil war, or if the PLO loses control of the security situation, and settlers are threatened, the Israeli Army will reserve the right to come in and crush the Palestinian forces. If needed, the Israelis do have nuclear weapons to defend themselves, should a larger Arab threat arise. Israel is the fourth leading nuclear power in the world, thus gaining a qualitative edge over any combination of Arab forces. The bottom line here is that the dreams of Palestinians for their future state would be set back for at least two more generations.

On the positive side, there are multiple dividends for both Palestinians and Israelis to make the peace process work, purely for their development as nations and out of self-interests.

A "Profitable" Withdrawal

For Israel, there are multiple reasons to embrace the peace process. Without a doubt, Rabin obtained the best deal and in the short run, he gained far more than he lost. He is giving up an ungovernable drain on his military machine and economy by unloading the Gaza Strip. The joke among Palestinians at the September 13 ceremony was that when the PLO was confronted with the proposal for Israel to give them the Gaza Strip, they answered: "Okay, what will you give us in exchange?"

Rabin and Israel have conceded little in the West Bank by surrendering the tiny city of Jericho and the Gaza Strip. Both areas will be surrounded by the Israeli Army that reserves the right to enter the areas when "necessary." Both areas are a financial and political burden on Israel. Meanwhile, Israel maintains control of the land, resources (especially water), the most strategic military regions, Jerusalem, the right to continue settlements, and is dealing with a PLO that represents no military threat to Israel. There are already indications that Israel will utilize the peace accord with the PLO to argue for more weapons, which, in fact, they have already done. The *Washington Post* reported on the eve of the agreement that Israel was about to purchase up to a billion dollars in new F-16 aircraft, adding to its arsenal of sophistocated weapons, giving it a qualitative edge over any combination of Arab armies.

At the same time, Israel realizes that in the long run it will need to shift its economic dependence away from the United States and develop treaties and economic alliances with the Arab world, a largely untapped market for high-quality electronics, agricultural, and other products. If Israel can in the long term significantly reduce the high percentage of the GNP that is presently devoted to the military, it could thrive economically. It is in the self-interests of Israel's future economic strength and security to see a successful Palestinian state, one that cooperates in tourism, shares resources, and creates a technological and economic miracle in the Holy Land. An enduring peace arrangement is the only vehicle that will ensure such a development.

Economic Development for Palestine

For Palestinians, the best-case scenario includes a gradual assumption of authority over the Gaza Strip and Jericho districts, with massive international financial investment.

Original projections by the PLO indicate that a minimum of $12 billion dollars over the next eight years (by 2001) will be necessary to make the plan viable. Additionally, the initial transfer of authority from the IDF to the Palestinian legislative body will need to begin within six to eight months of the signing. In early October 1993 there were indications that several European nations will be joined by Japan and the United States to pledge the initial three-to-five billion dollars for the first twelve months (through December 1994). But the devastation of the Gaza and West Bank economy may be far more catastrophic when analysts realize what more than twenty-five years of military occupation have done.

Just one brief example is that in Gaza, according to the United Nations, over five-hundred thousand Palestinians are totally dependent on the meager income of the thirty-to-forty-thousand wage laborers who migrate to work in Israel each day. Thus three-fourths of the Gaza population are dependent on these jobs that are often canceled without notice when the army places Gaza under curfew. It is estimated that $750,000 is lost each day when this happens.

Nevertheless, announcements have been made of a December 12, 1993, Israeli withdrawal from the Gaza Strip and Jericho, while Mr. Arafat and his leadership will establish headquarters in Jericho on January 1, 1994. If these projections move forward on schedule, if the desperately needed economic relief and quality of life begin to change immediately, the PLO will maintain control and carry the momentum to its side in the struggle with the opposition. If there are major delays and internal or external complications, then the PLO will lose all credibility and the frustrations will inevitably lead to violence.

The Palestinians must also act quickly to implement various forms of democratization, within the society at large and within the PLO itself. The PLO has from its inception embraced a vision for a democratic movement and called for a secular democratic state. It needs to stay on course in this endeavor toward democratizaton.

The Palestinian gains of a degree of international legitimacy, the possibility of elections, some economic relief, and the first opportunity in their modern history to rebuild their community on their own soil, are beneficial gains. The interim solution is a clear compromise as it will represent a tiny Palestinian entity confederated with Jordan, with a limit of five years. During this period various strategies will be employed to expand control over the entire West Bank (and Gaza Strip) as Palestinians prepare themselves for "independence and self-rule." As most Palestinians told us: "It's not much, but it is a start. Now let's see what we can do together to make it thrive."

8

The Importance of Prayer

Pray for the peace of Jerusalem: "May those who love you be secure. May there be peace within your walls and security within your citadels."

PSALM 122:6-7

Although Christians may not completely agree on how the accord fits into God's plan, we *do* agree on the need to support such developments with prayer. As Dr. Joe Aldrich, president of Multnomah Bible College recently told us, "Christians should thank the Lord for this peace accord. . . . As long as the peace accord lasts, we have more time to work for the Savior who wants to bring others to himself."

It is important to remember that all the children of Abraham—Christians, Jews, and Muslims—are God's concern. War in the Holy Land is always tragic for the way it desecrates holy sites, but worse is the loss of life among God's people. If we really believe that people who do not confess Christ are "lost," then the prospect of continued killing ought to compel every Christian to support every effort to bring peace to this region.

Unfortunately, few American Christians realize that there is a dynamic Christian community among the Palestinians. These "forgotten Christians" have been unknown in the West until recently. Their numbers have diminished considerably since the establishment of Israel (in 1948), and

71

severe conditions have caused massive Christian emigration. Some fear that within a generation there will be no visible Palestinian Christian community in the Holy Land, only empty shrines and museums to remind us that one day a church was there. We in the West must work now to reverse this coming tragedy, but more on this in part 3.

Almost as soon as the accord was signed, Christian leaders in the United States and around the world weighed in with their responses. *Christianity Today's* October 4 lead editorial, written by executive editor, David Neff, reminded Christians—evangelicals in particular—"to pray for those who have yet to settle these issues." It then lists four major areas on which Christians should focus their prayers:

- Pray for clearly defined territorial responsibility and respect for territorial integrity (including Jerusalem). Ask God for justice for displaced Palestinian families.

- Absolute fairness is impossible. But generosity in this situation requires the watching world, both the West and Arab nations, to become the helping world: to finance acceptable housing, schools, and hospitals in order to foster an adequate standard of living. Continued unemployment and poverty will only contribute to further instability in the region.

- Pray for Israeli security. The multiple wars of aggression Israel has suffered during its four-and-one-half decades means that that country has a justifiably edgy populace. Unfortunately, that edginess has resulted in human-rights violations and the creation of a population of refugees. Now, however, optimism is dominant. Pray that their optimism is well-founded.

- Remember Palestinian Christians, most of whom are Orthodox or Anglican. Thank God for this easing of tensions. Now, it seems, God has worked in his own mysteriously slow way to bring about this miracle.

- Pray that Christians will be able to take appropriate leadership roles and strengthen the new atmosphere of peace and hope.

The Washington, D.C.-based group, Churches for a Middle East Peace, issued a joint statement on the day of the signing that said in part: "Today's declaration should be a source of hope for Israelis living in fear and for Palestinians living under an oppressive occupation."

Most Protestant and Roman Catholic denominations viewed the agreement as a "heroic step" in the "long and arduous journey" toward peace (Disciples of Christ president Richard Hamm). The American Jewish Committee's spokesman, A. James Rudin, was "optimistic and cautious," reminding us that "the ultimate test is not in words but deeds."

Palestinian Christians generally celebrated the accord but reflected their deep concern about the future. Bishop Samir Kafity, the first Palestinian to become the Anglican bishop in Jerusalem and the Middle East, issued an official statement after the signing stating:

Tonight we celebrate, both Palestinian and Israeli, together with the multitude of people who care for peace and justice, the inauguration of the journey of peace.

That journey, starting today from Jericho and Gaza, will undoubtedly reach all of the towns and cities in the Palestinian territories. Together with our neighbors, Israel, Jordan, Syria, and Lebanon, we look forward to a new era of justice and peace in the Middle East. . . . We shall continue to pray here in St. George's Cathedral (Jerusalem) with our Muslim and Jewish sisters and brothers for God's blessing on this journey of peace: a prayer that all the peoples of this region might live in the perfect image of God. . . . "Blessed are the peacemakers, for they shall be called the children of God."

The Middle East Council of Churches (MECC), the ecumenical umbrella under which most of the fourteen-million Christians of the Middle East stand, issued their statement from General Secretary Mr. Gabriel Habib and the executive committee (comprised of Catholic, Eastern Orthodox, Oriental Orthodox, and Arab Evangelical Churches) on September 14:

> We view the present PLO/Israeli agreement in Washington as a sign of hope and a turning point in the history of the Middle East and particularly in the Palestinian-Israeli relationships. . . . Moreover, as we witness this miracle of transformation from a past of fear and war into a future of possible mutual trust for peace, we wish to affirm once again the centrality of Jerusalem for all peoples and religious communities concerned.

> In this regard we reject all attempts for exclusive control over the city by any religious or political entity and long for genuine partnership between Judaism, Christianity, and Islam in defining the destiny of the Holy City of peace. Therefore, we appeal to all churches worldwide to pray that the new era of mutual recognition between the two peoples would restore the dignity of all Palestinians inside and outside their occupied territories and would safeguard and even deepen their unity in their struggle for their right of self-determination. "Let thy work be manifest to thy servants, and thy glorious power to their children" (Psalm 90:16 RSV).

The MECC statement reflects accurately the commitment of the fourteen million Christians, who have suffered wars and threats of persecution since the first century, to peace and coexistence with their Jewish and Muslim neighbors. Representative of this prayer for peace is their prayer and concern for Jerusalem, that it truly be a city for everyone and not the exclusive domain of one party. Their call for prayer worldwide will hopefully be heeded by Christians on every continent.

Even as Christians acknowledge these calls from their leaders to pray for the peace accord and the way it is implemented, one question keeps cropping up, especially among American evangelicals: How does this all fit into God's plan? In the next part, we will show how some are attempting to answer that provocative question.

Part III
What It Means

by Dan O'Neill and Don Wagner

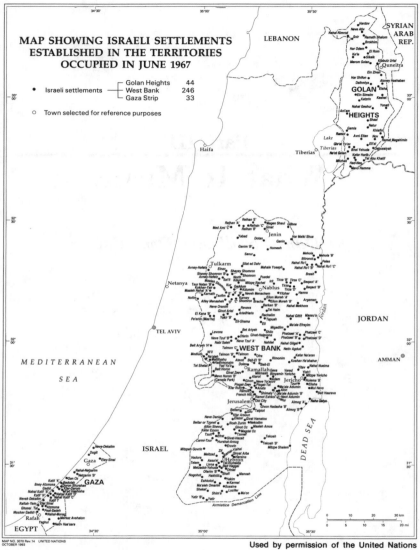

**MAP SHOWING ISRAELI SETTLEMENTS
ESTABLISHED IN THE TERRITORIES
OCCUPIED IN JUNE 1967**

• Israeli settlements	Golan Heights	44
	West Bank	246
	Gaza Strip	33

○ Town selected for reference purposes

LEBANON

SYRIAN ARAB REP.

GOLAN HEIGHTS

Haifa

Lake Tiberias

Tiberias

Jenin

Tulkarm

Netanya

Nablus

MEDITERRANEAN SEA

TEL AVIV

WEST BANK

JORDAN

AMMAN

Ramallah

Jericho

Jerusalem

DEAD SEA

ISRAEL

Gaza

GAZA

Hebron

Rafah

EGYPT

Armistice Demarcation Line

0   10   20   30 km
0   5   10   15   20 mi

9

The Israeli-Christian Connection

Take heed that no one leads you astray. For many will come in my name saying, "I am the Christ," and they will lead many astray. And you will hear of wars and rumors of wars; see that you are not alarmed; for this must take place, but the end is not yet. For nation will rise against nation, and kingdom against kingdom, and there will be famines and earthquakes in various places: all this is but the beginning of the birthpangs.
MATTHEW 24:4–8 RSV

*P*rophecy experts are scratching their heads. Sweeping changes on the world scene just do not make sense. At least not as clearly as they once did. The Soviet Union no longer exists. The Russian Federation is so weak that it is a threat only to itself. And now Israel is shaking hands with its arch enemy— the PLO and Yasser Arafat. Those who predicted a Soviet attack on Israel according to Ezekiel 38–39 now realize that is unlikely, at least in the near future. This is a far cry from the prophetic zeal expressed by many Christian leaders when the Soviet Union was a strong and aggressive supporter of the Arab states. Consider, for example, the following statement from the Reverend Chuck Smith, pastor of the fifteen-thousand member Calvary Chapel in Southern California:

[Russian invasion of Israel?] That excites me because if war breaks out—and it's certainly within the realm of probability—very soon we could be rejoicing around the throne of God in glory! (*End Times,* Chuck Smith, Maranatha House, 1978).

If we scroll back the pages of history to 1948, we can quickly understand why such glee could be expressed by Christians. The establishment of Israel in 1948 caused even liberal theologians to rejoice, for different theological reasons. The seminal liberal theologian of the post-World War II era, Dr. Reinhold Niebuhr of Union Theological Seminary in New York, celebrated the birth of Israel as a triumph of justice and liberation. A stream of contemporary liberal Christian supporters of Zionist theology continues in the work of Dr. Franklin Littell of Temple University, the former "Death of God" theologian Paul Van Buren, and the Roman Catholic Holocaust theologian Fr. John Pawlikowski.

The evangelical world viewed the birth of Israel as the fulfillment of biblical prophecy and the first clear sign that the final countdown to Armageddon had begun. In his bestselling book, *The Late, Great Planet Earth,* author Hal Lindsey wrote:

But the most important sign in Matthew has to be the restoration of the Jews to the land in the rebirth of Israel. . . . When the Jewish people, after nearly 2000 years of exile, under relentless persecution, became a nation again on 14 May 1948, the "fig tree" put forth its first leaves (Lindsey, *The Late Great Planet Earth,* Zondervan, 1970).

Viewing the birth of Israel in 1948 as the fulfillment of biblical prophecy was the dominant perspective on the Middle East within most of the American evangelical community for nearly three decades. The amazing victory of

Israel over Arab armies in June 1967, and especially the capture of Jerusalem, seemed to confirm the prophetic scenario. L. Nelson Bell, Billy Graham's father-in-law and editor of the influential *Christianity Today*, wrote the following immediately after Israel's 1967 victory:

> That for the first time in more than 2000 years Jerusalem is now completely in the hands of the Jews gives the student of the Bible a thrill and a renewed faith in the accuracy and validity of the Bible (*Christianity Today*, July 21, 1967).

As evangelicals who grew up in Christian dispensational traditions, we both subscribed to this view. As Bible-believing Christians, we understood that we could hold no other position.

The October War of 1973 seemed to confirm the predictions that Hal Lindsey's *Late Great Planet Earth* had proposed two years earlier. It appeared that Lindsey and others had been divinely inspired in their anticipation of the events of October 1973, which added to the appeal of Armageddon theology.

By the late 1970s, following Israel's election of Menachem Begin's Likud government, this theology began to be translated into political strategies for several groups, the most noteworthy being Jerry Falwell's "Moral Majority." Televangelists such as Pat Robertson, Jim and Tammy Bakker, Mike Evans, Paul Crouch, and James Robison were among those who promoted the pro-Israel support network.

During these years, four currents seemed to be converging in the religious and political scenes:

1. President Jimmy Carter, Southern Baptist Sunday school teacher from Plains, Georgia, shocked and disappointed the fundamentalists and charismatics with his human-rights agenda and newly announced concern for Palestin-

ians. After Carter used the words "Palestinian homeland" in a speech in March 1977, full-page advertisements began to appear in dozens of newspapers across the United States. Signed by a list of prominent evangelicals, the advertisement stated in part: "The time has come for evangelicals to affirm their belief in biblical prophecy and Israel's divine right to the Holy Land" ("Evangelicals' Concern for Israel," Paid Advertisement, the *Christian Science Monitor,* November 3, 1977).

The heavily financed campaign bore fruit for the emerging evangelical Christian political alliance with pro-Israeli lobbies in the United States and the Israeli government itself. This phase also marked the beginning of Jimmy Carter's loss of conservative Christian support. As Jerry Strober, a former American-Jewish Committee employee under contract to organize the campaign later told the *Washington Post*:

> [The evangelicals] are Carter's constituency, and he had better listen to them. . . . The real source of strength the Jews have in this country is from the Evangelicals. (William Claibourne, "Israelis Look on U.S. Evangelicals as Potent Ally," *Washington Post,* March 23, 1981.)

2. Begin's Likud party used the same biblical language that we evangelicals found in our Scofield Bibles for Israel and the occupied territories of Judea and Samaria. A literalistic biblical match was in the making. During this period many of the major Zionist organizations deemphasized their efforts with mainline Protestant denominations and shifted to the pro-Israel wing of evangelicalism. The late Rabbi Marc Tannenbaum, the American-Jewish Committee's national interreligious affairs director, summarized the change in this way:

The evangelical community is the largest and fastest growing block of pro-Israeli, pro-Jewish sentiment in this country. Since the 1967 War, the Jewish community has felt abandoned by Protestants, by groups clustered around the National Council of Churches, which because of sympathy with Third-World causes, gave the impression of support for the PLO. There was a vacuum in public support to Israel that began to be filled by the fundamentalists and evangelical Christians (The *Washington Post*, March 23, 1981).

3. Evangelicals were now a political force with a potential of fifty-to-sixty million Americans. We became one of the key target communities for the powerful Israeli lobby. We also had money and large mailing lists; money from several of America's wealthiest individuals, such as the Hunt family, and the direct-mail technology from one of its pioneers, Richard Viguerie.

4. Israel began to accelerate its tours, special briefings, and educational efforts for evangelicals. One noteworthy educational project came when then president of the Southern Baptist Convention, the Reverend Bailey Smith, stated that "God does not hear the prayers of Jews." After severe criticism from American-Jewish leaders, Smith agreed to go on a quick tour to Israel. He returned a changed man and was soon a true "Friend of Israel."

This political convergence could be seen in 1979, when Menachem Begin presented the Reverend Falwell with the prestigious Jabotinsky Award from the government of Israel in appreciation for Falwell's support and then donated a Lear jet for his travels. After bombing Iraq's nuclear reactor in 1981, Begin did not call President Reagan first. He telephoned Jerry Falwell and asked him to "tell America why Israel needed to protect herself." The syndicated columnists Evans and Novak noted in August, 1981, that Falwell's ties to Begin were so close that before meeting even Arab Christians, the evangelist telephoned the prime minister in order to seek his advice (Rowland Evans and Robert Novak, "Falwell-Begin Ties," *Dallas Times Herald,* August 7, 1981).

When Israel invaded Lebanon on June 6, 1982, CBN's Pat Robertson charted Israeli attacks each day on his CBN "700 Club" and interpreted events according to the end times fulfillment of biblical prophecy. (Don's mother, a longtime financial supporter of Pat Robertson and an advocate of his views, became confused when she realized that her son was under the Israeli bombardment for that first week). Robertson believed the invasion of Lebanon was a sign pointing toward the Battle of Armageddon and claimed that Israel's attack was a "modern Joshua event." He urged television viewers to write or call President Reagan immediately, hoping he would encourage Israel's war against the Palestinians.

Hindsight always has the benefit of clearer vision, so it would be unfair to declare our unswerving allegiance to Israel to have been wrong. Despite a minority of Christians who warned against favoring the secular state of Israel over their Christian brothers and sisters in Palestinian communities, the events seemed to give credence to those who saw Armageddon just around the corner.

Whether the final battle is near or not, one question must still be answered: How should we respond to Christians in the Arab world?

10

Christian Arabs?

One of the best ways to understand how the accord fits into God's plan is to develop relationships throughout the Middle East with all of God's peoples. In 1986, Don Wagner and Dr. Ray Bakke, then the Lausanne Committee on World Evangelization's specialist on large cities, took a quiet "listening tour" to six Arab countries and Israel. The three priorities they heard most frequently were:

"Please do something about the Palestinian issue in relation to your own government."

"Please help us understand the evangelical mission groups coming into our region and let them know who we are," and,

"Please stand with us while our churches are dying."

In a meeting with King Hussein of Jordan, Ray and Don were discussing the future of the Christian community in the Middle East when the king, a Muslim, expressed his deep concern over the exodus of Christians and told them: "I believe that in many ways the Arab Christians are the glue that holds our societies together."

As American Christians learn more about Christians in the Middle East, the prophetic questions tend to pale compared to issues of evangelism, witness, and the life of the church. Thankfully, more and more Christians have found ways to make contact with their counterparts in the Holy Land, as the following brief account suggests.

The year 1982 was a turning point for American
evangelicals and the beginning of a process that continues
today. In 1979 and 1981, a group of evangelical Christians
issued the LaGrange Declaration, which called on the U.S.
evangelical community to continue its commitment to Israel
but to consider the case of the Palestinians. The declaration
was signed by over five thousand Christians but did not
receive broad circulation in evangelical journals and major
organizations. It did, however, awaken many to a different
Christian interpretation of the Holy Land, and awareness of
the forgotten factor—the Palestinian Christian community.
The declaration stated in part:

> We address this urgent call to the Church of Jesus Christ
> to hear and heed those voices crying out as bruised reeds
> for justice in the land where our Lord walked, taught, was
> crucified, and rose from the dead.
>
> We have closed our hearts to these voices and isolated
> ourselves even from the pleading of fellow Christians who
> continue to live in that land (the LaGrange Declaration,
> (*Sojourners Magazine,* July, 1979).

In 1982, the organization for which we work, Mercy
Corps International, launched a series of educational tours
of the Middle East for North American evangelical leaders.
They met Arab Christians, Muslims, and Jewish leaders from
the religious and political eschelons, both in Israel and in the
Occupied Territories. Several tours included stops in Lebanon, Syria, and Jordan or Egypt as well. Over a ten-year
period, Mercy Corps took twenty-one delegations of leaders
to the Middle East. The tours were in direct contrast to the
usual Holy Land tour that did not provide contacts with

Arab Christians but concentrated on Israel and the biblical sites.

Other evangelical organizations were sensing God's leading to modify their positions on the Holy Land and the Middle East. World Vision International was among them. As one of the largest and most influential relief agencies in the world, World Vision has had a strong record of involvement with the poor but had been slow to become involved in the Middle East. With Beirut under siege in June 1982, and Lebanon's southern population cut off from food and other supplies, World Vision along with other agencies waited two weeks to bring needed food and medicine into the South. The late Stan Mooneyham, then president of World Vision, flew to Beirut and joined Len Rodgers, the Middle East director, and together they took the first convoy into the devastated Palestinian refugee camps near the biblical cities of Tyre and Sidon. Mooneyham and Rodgers then issued a strong protest that was covered in both the religious and secular press stating what they had seen: over 50 percent of the camps leveled; most of the male population over fourteen in prison; and massive starvation.

Prime Minister Begin was furious with the World Vision protest. Several of Begin's evangelical friends were contacted to bring pressure on World Vision to retract its views, but Mooneyham remained firm in what he had seen with his eyes and felt in his heart, and World Vision paid a dear price in lost donors.

At the same time, evangelical periodicals like *Christianity Today* began to raise concerns about the situation. After touring Israel and the West Bank, editor-in-chief Gil Beers and associate editor Tom Minnery wrote editorials and provided the opportunity for the respected Quaker evangelical, Dr. Landrum Bolling, to write a feature article on the Middle East. A lead editorial by Harry Genet called for a just solution to the Palestine question and challenged the Reagan administration's Middle East policy. The *Christianity Today* issue signaled that it was no longer taboo for evangelicals to be critical of Israel's policies and raised significant questions about justice in the Holy Land.

A final source of change, and perhaps the most important, was the considerable role played by Arab Christians themselves. Among the many leaders who have given tirelessly of their hospitality and Christian love, we mention only three:

In 1983, Father Elias Chacour of the Galilean village Ibillin published his remarkable spiritual autobiography, *Blood Brothers,* with Zondervan Publishing House/Chosen Books. Perhaps more than any previous book, Fr. Chacour's *Blood Brothers* touched the hearts and opened the minds of thousands of evangelicals concerning Christians in the Holy Land. Since the book was published, many thousands have visited and volunteered at Prophet Elias High School and have been inspired by Fr. Chacour's vision. Among them are former Secretary of State James Baker and his wife, Susan.

Jonathan and Beth Kuttab are a second force for changing attitudes among American Christians. Beth is an American from Pennsylvania, and Jonathan a Jerusalem-born son of a Palestinian evangelical pastor. They met at Messiah College, where they received their undergraduate degrees. Jonathan also graduated from the University of Virginia Law School and is a highly skilled human-rights attorney and lay theologian. He has been a frequent speaker in evangelical colleges, on ABC-TV's "Nightline," and has met with thousands of visitors in his land. Jonathan and Beth Kuttab have also given generously of their time to introduce Western Christians to the issues of Palestine and Israel. Jonathan's cousin, Reverend Bishara Awad, is director of the evangelically oriented Bethlehem Bible College.

A third leader is Gabriel Habib, a Lebanese Christian who is the general secretary (CEO) of the Middle East Council of Churches (MECC). Trained as a lawyer and influenced by the Orthodox youth movement in the 1960s, Gabi Habib has become a pioneer in bringing the once-fragmented churches of the Middle East into the unity of one body of Jesus Christ. Despite the fact that MECC is only twenty years old, Mr. Habib and his colleagues have the only regional church council in which the Eastern Orthodox, Oriental Orthodox, Catholics (Roman, Maronite, and Melkite), Protestants [Anglican, National Evangelical, and Lutheran] have united in one family. He also organized the first Christian conference in history on the question of Palestine.

One more organization deserves mention: Evangelicals for Middle East Understanding (EMEU). Launched in London in 1986 with the help of Dr. John Stott, EMEU has held a series of small annual meetings between 1987 and 1990, and decided in 1991 to convene an invitation-only conference for evangelical leaders on the island of Cyprus. Cosponsored with the Middle East Council of Churches, the conference drew over ninety Western evangelical leaders, representing fifty-five different mission agencies, churches, and organizations. From the Middle East there were over fifty delegates, most selected by their bishops or regional authority. They came from the Gulf area, Iraq, Syria, Lebanon, Egypt, Israel, Jordan, and Palestine. The deep spiritual and theological fellowship was inspiring and challenging.

Evangelicals discovered the Arab Christians to be Bible-believing sisters and brothers whose conservative theology and lifestyles matched their own. Arab Christians discovered that the evangelicals had not abandoned them. They simply did not know them—and now even that oversight was changing. The conference was so successful that it was repeated in 1992 with the same inspiring results. In February 1994, the venue will shift to the United States.

These developments and many others signal that the Holy Spirit is bringing about a slow change within Western evangelical Christianity concerning the Middle East. This opinion is confirmed by a poll conducted by *Christianity Today* (March 9, 1992), which indicated that 46 percent of evangelicals surveyed had changed their attitude concerning Israel during the previous decade. Of those surveyed, 39 percent said they were "more critical" of Israel, whereas only 12 percent said they were "more accepting." An overwhelming 88 percent now believe that "Christians should hold the state of Israel to the same standards of justice and human rights in international and internal affairs as any other state."

For the sake of the Palestinian church, we hope this change in attitude is not too late. The exodus of Palestinian Christians from the Holy Land since the birth of Israel in 1948 has been shocking. Perhaps the most graphic illustration is in Jerusalem where in 1922, Jerusalem had 28,607 inhabitants, of which 14,699 (51 percent) were Christians, according to the (British) Mandatory Government's statistics. By 1978 the Israeli Bureau of Statistics counted only 10,191 Christians out of 93,509 residents in Arab East Jerusalem, or less than 10 percent of the total. Dr. Bernard Sabella of Bethlehem University has been monitoring these statistics and his data indicates the numbers are now under 7000 Christians [See Donald E. Wagner, "Holy Land Christians Worry About Survival," *The Christian Century*, April 24, 1991].

What is so demoralizing about these statistics is that by natural birth rate the Palestinian Christian community in Jerusalem should be in the neighborhood of fifty-to-sixty thousand, given the 51-percent statistic of 1922. This phenomenal turnaround is alarming indeed when one realizes that it is true throughout the West Bank and the entire Middle East.

In Bethlehem, which prior to 1967 was a predominantly Christian city, the Christian population is now down to approximately 40 percent of the total. Where have they gone? There are more Palestinian Christians from Bethlehem living in Chile and Brazil than in Bethlehem. Or consider Ramallah, a larger Christian city just north of Jerusalem. Its Christian population has also dropped, with more Ramallahites living in Detroit, Michigan, and Jacksonville, Florida than in Ramallah.

We state this concern not to raise the issue of tension between Christians and Muslims—quite to the contrary. Christians are not leaving Palestine for that reason, because it has never been an issue in Palestine. Christians and Muslims have long lived in harmony. There are other reasons. As Gabriel Habib of the Middle East Council of Churches recently described the exodus across the region: "Fear, human suffering, and hopelessness have now caused profound concern about the very continuity of Christian presence and witness in this region."

The Anglican bishop of Jerusalem in exile, Elia Khouri, sadly told us: "I give Christianity ten-to fifteen years in Jordan and the West Bank, no more." The prominent Israeli author Amos Elon said that Jerusalem may soon become a mere museum for tourists, "bereft of Christianity as a living religion." Local Christians call it the "museumification of Christianity in the Holy Land," for in a few years Western Christian pilgrims will see only empty buildings and no living church.

But despite these and other pressures, a remnant of committed Palestinian Christians are choosing to remain. They view their lives as ministries as they are called by God to be vehicles of healing reconciliation between Jews and

Muslims, and faithful witnesses of the Gospel in the land of Jesus. Many Christian leaders are urging their people to stay and are asking Western friends to assist them, a type of Macedonian call and "collection for the Christians in Jerusalem" (and all the Holy Land).

Will we, the American church, heed their call?

11

What Christian Leaders Are Saying About the Accord

Even before the signing of the peace accord, evangelical author David Hunt predicted a "temporary peace" in the Middle East, "that will, in fact, be of the Antichrist." Hunt continues: "That (temporary) peace will be guaranteed by the Antichrist and will ultimately lead to the most destructive war in the earth's history. Sadly, one day soon and precisely as prophesied, all the nations of the world will bring their armies against Israel to destroy her people." (David Hunt, *How Close Are We?* Harvest House Publishers, 1993).

Hunt goes on to note that despite Israel's mistreatment of the Palestinians, these "imperfections are beside the point" (p. 44). God will keep the prophetic schedule to be culminated in the Battle of Armageddon, with the promises to Abraham, Isaac, and Jacob remaining in force.

Hunt reflects the views of many evangelical Christians and sets the tone for how they might view the present Middle East Peace Accord. Is this the "false peace" of the Antichrist? Or perhaps it is a forerunner that will prepare the way for even bolder moves by the Antichrist.

In an effort to ascertain how a variety of U.S.-based evangelicals from different perspectives were viewing the

peace accord, we surveyed several leaders immediately
following the signing of the accord. Two questions were put
before each leader or organization:

1. How should Christians respond to the recent Israeli-
   PLO peace accord?
2. From your understanding of biblical prophecy, how
   does the recent peace accord fit into God's plan?

We also followed press reports and the broadcasts of
some of the major televangelists to add to the mix of
responses.

For example, immediately after the signing of the accord,
Pat Robertson on the "700 Club" said he felt this was indeed
a part of God's plan.

Best-selling author Benny Hinn was more direct. On
October 3 he told his television audience that the September
13 accord was a direct fulfillment of prophecy and that
young people in the audience definitely would not need to
purchase cemetery plots because Jesus would return in their
lifetimes.

That view differs from that of Dallas Theological
Seminary professor, Charles Dyer, who told the Associated
Press that he did not think the accord fulfilled any particular
biblical passage but added, "My personal feeling is that it
could be part of the setting of the end-stage events."

Paige Patterson, president of Southeastern Baptist Seminary, said, "I don't care what anyone thinks of Yasser Arafat,
he is not the Antichrist." But he goes on to say that by giving
up territory, Israel could become strategically weakened,
vulnerable to the "driving out" referred to in the ninth
chapter of Daniel.

Entertainer Pat Boone, presently the official "Christian
ambassador of tourism for Israel," (appointed by the govern-

ment of Israel) and a careful follower of biblical prophecy, is very concerned about the current situation.

> From my understanding of biblical prophecy, the Is-
> raeli/PLO Peace Accord is part of God's plan. After all,
> Jesus said early in his ministry, "Blessed are the peace-
> makers," and the leaders of Israel today have taken the
> lead in negotiating this plan. Further, on all my trips to
> Israel and in every press interview, I've said, "God doesn't
> just have a plan for Israel but for the whole Middle East.
> Violence is not the answer, and if we'll take time to find
> out what God's plan is, it will benefit everybody."

In response to the question on Biblical prophecy, Boone said:

> In light of Isaiah 19, when Syria, Jordan and Egypt all
> decide, in concert with Israel and the PLO, that a new
> highway from Egypt up through the Golan Heights and on
> to Damascus is a timely and beneficial undertaking—we'll
> know we're living in the last period of history!
>
> . . .as long as the negotiations are peaceful, and the object
> on both sides is to obtain a fair and workable and above
> all, peaceful resolution, Christians should applaud and
> promote it. We're commanded to "pray for the peace of
> Jerusalem," and it appears our prayers are being answered,
> at least for now. As the officially appointed Christian
> ambassador for tourism for Israel, I'm praying for this
> accord with special fervor.

From Tuvya Zaretsky, director of the Southern California District of Jews for Jesus came this response:

> As a Jewish Christian writing on the eve of Sukkot, there
> is an awareness of the prophetic promises that in God's
> plan the city of Jerusalem will be a place of ingathering
> (Zecheriah 14:9–16). That cannot happen until the curse
> of Deuteronomy 28 is removed and God himself draws

the Jewish people back to the land of Israel at the end of days according to His plan.

If the "curse" of Zechariah 14:11 is that curse (Deuteronomy 28), then it can be seen in connection with the necessary restoration of the Jewish people at some time. It cannot be determined in advance. . . . Having said that, how can anyone attribute the recent peace accord between Israel and the PLO to the plan of God? The affairs of contemporary political statehood will all ultimately serve the purposes of God.

These statements by evangelicals who would be considered supportive of "Armageddon theology" take a cautiously open approach, suggesting that God might be at work in this process. But most also warn against viewing this as a clear prophetic sign, while maintaining the future fulfillment hermeneutic. Contrast this to a typical interpretation made by Dr. John Walvoord, one of the leading theologians of the dispensational school, immediately after the 1973 war—a statement he updated in 1990 after Saddam Hussein entered Kuwait:

A peace settlement in the Middle East is one of the most important events predicted for the end times. The signing of this peace treaty will start the final countdown leading to Armageddon and then introduce the new world leader who will be destined to become world dictator—the infamous Anti-Christ. According to Daniel 9:27, the last seven years leading up to the Second Coming of Christ will begin with just such a peace settlement (*Armageddon, Oil, and the Middle East Crisis,* Zondervan Publishing House, 1974).

While we did receive responses that reflected the traditional Lindsey and Walvoord premillenialist dispensational theology, they did not dominate the responses.

Among *some* televangelists, the Antichrist is believed to be at work in the peace accord in order to deceive Israel and the church. In the Antichrist scenario as taught by Lindsey and Walvoord, the Antichrist is a "new world dictator" who will first reveal himself in the role "of a peacemaker in the Middle East. This event will take place during the first stage of the revived Roman Empire, the fourth empire described by Daniel" (Dan. 7:8; (Walvoord).

We expect that this view will continue to be the opinion of many hardened dispensationalists, but we hear change occurring among those leaders with direct Middle East experience. If however, the peace accord breaks down and Israel's security is threatened, we expect that those beginning to open up to this peace as part of God's overarching will, will obviously revert back to the dispensational theology, which thrives on war and conflict.

Evangelical author and futurist, Tom Sine, represented a "middle ground" evangelical view popular among a growing number of church leaders:

> I feel that many evangelicals and charismatics are asking the wrong questions about current events. Instead of asking, "When is it all going to go boom?" they should be asking, "What are God's purposes in this situation?" I believe we should agree that God's purposes include peace, beating swords into plowshares, and rejoicing when the lion lies with the lamb. We should be celebrating and encouraging the amazing events now unfolding in the Holy Land.

Sine believes that if the lion can lie down with the lamb in the millennium, should that not be God's purpose today? As Christians, we should be seeking this same reality now, which strikes at the heart of Jesus' message throughout the Gospel.

This view was echoed by Bill Warnock, director of World Vision's Jerusalem office:

> I believe God's plan is well-summarized in John 3:16, and in Jesus' announcement: "The Kingdom of God is at hand. Repent, believe the Good News." Anything which promotes peace and justice is a move toward the realization of the Kingdom of God. Israel and Palestine have both suffered the evil effects of the occupation, albeit in different ways. This step of mutual recognition between the PLO and Israel is a giant step but still the first of many steps which must follow if a true peace is to come.

As for the accord in light of biblical prophecy, Warnock offered this personal interpretation:

> All prophecy in the Old Testament must be interpreted in the light of Christ, the Word of God. Although I grew up with the Scofield Bible, I have great difficulty with the dispensationalist interpretation of selected passages of the Old Testament as referring to a return of the Jews in our time. This is especially true after what I've experienced living here in Jerusalem for the past six years. Jesus was very clear in making the Kingdom open to all and in breaking down the dividing wall between Jew and Gentile. Nowhere in the New Testament is the restoration of the Jewish state or the promise of the land repeated.

In summary, how the accord fits into God's plan depends, in part, on how one reads Scripture. For most dispensationalists and others who believe that the establishment of the modern state of Israel in 1948 set the stage for a gradual winding down toward a final Armageddon battle, the accord clearly suggests that we may be moving closer toward the end of history.

For those who do not equate the modern state of Israel with the Jewish people whom God favored, the accord is indeed under God's sovereign plans for humankind but probably not an indicator of the "last times."

Interestingly, Christians of all theological leanings have emphasized the need for prayer. Clearly, God is at work in the Holy Land, presenting the church with unprecedented opportunities for witness. As evangelist Billy Graham told the Associated Press, "I can't tell you how the events are going to take place. . . . Nor would I say that we are at the end of the age. But I can't help but believe in my heart that we are moving toward some climax in history."

12

What the Bible Teaches

W*e are well aware that the Bible*—indeed, the holy writings of any religion—is often used to batter people into accepting a personal political viewpoint. As we conclude this book, we hope our own biblical views come from honest searching and not from a personal mission to advance a particular cause. As we have reported, we both grew up in a dispensationalist tradition and still carry the deep love of Israel that this perspective teaches. But it was also the dispensational high view of Scripture that encouraged us to approach the Holy Land with our Bibles (and minds) open.

So what follows is an attempt to look at the accord in the larger context of the Bible's teaching about Israel, the Jews, and followers of Christ. We hope our thoughts will prompt dialogue and challenge you to listen more closely to God's word. If this happens, we praise God.

Covenant

According to Genesis 12:1–3 (also 15:1–7 and 17–21; and 17:1–14) the land we call "holy" was given to the children of Abraham as a gift within the context of the covenant with Yahweh. In the Bible, there are four essential ingredients of a covenant (*be'rith* in Hebrew). First, God is the initiator of the covenant relationship and the people are the recipients. God establishes the terms of behavior, and we respond, hopefully in faithfulness. In the Abrahamic covenant, Yahweh called Abram and Sarah out of Ur of the Chaldees (Iraq today) and brought them to Canaan, a land occupied by various Semitic tribes.

Second, God's choice of Abram was not based on merit, spirituality, or any skills as far as we can tell from the texts. Abram, renamed Abraham, was selected from all the peoples of the region at that time as an act of God's grace, or as the Bible defines grace, "unmerited favor" (Ephesians 2:8–10 RSV, "for by grace you have been saved by through faith; and this is not your own doing, it is the gift of God).

Third, Abraham and Sarah responded in faith and obedience, the standards of behavior for all biblical covenants. Christians see Abraham as the model of faith because of his obedience, responding to God's call but "not knowing where he was to go" (Hebrews 11:8–22). Muslims and Jews also see Abraham as the model of faith. For Muslims, the Dome of the Rock is built over the rock of Mt. Moriah where Abraham nearly sacrificed Isaac (Genesis 22), and is the place where the Prophet Mohammed journeyed on his night ride with Allah before ascending to heaven. The Al Aqsa Mosque, which sits beside the Dome of the Rock shrine, represents the third holiest site in Islam. This reverence for Abraham in the three religions offers common ground for faith and coexistence, if we choose to use it.

Fourth, God provides certain instruments through which the covenant is to be lived. In Genesis, God gives Abraham and his descendants (including Ishmael, for the promise is first given before he is born) at least four instruments: land, election, descendants as numerous as sand in the sea, and making their name great among the nations (Genesis 12 and 17). All of these instruments were gifts from Yahweh and supplied only for the purpose that the faithful people will be "blessed" in order to "be a blessing to others." If they are not faithful, they are warned later, they can lose such instruments as the land, for they will be "vomited out" as were previous inhabitants (Leviticus 18:25).

To summarize, God grants the descendants of Abraham a unique relationship of faith and grace that demands covenant obedience. God will provide "blessings" (gifts) such as land and numerous descendants, but the purpose is to glorify God and not to become ends unto themselves. There is the danger that Israel and all nations have in relation to land and their nationalism. It becomes an exclusive expression of power often at the expense of others.

Land

There is no issue in the Middle East as sensitive as the land question. In this brief space we can only suggest certain themes that flow from the foundation we have established in the concept of the biblical covenant. Land in Scripture is never an end unto itself. It is a "gift" of God's grace, and the people are stewards or caretakers. In Leviticus 25:23 we read: "The land shall not be sold in perpetuity, for the land is mine; with me you are but aliens and tenants" (NRSV).

As such, the land is not declared holy in and of itself. Only God is holy, and faithful people might warrant the adjective if they are obedient: "You shall be holy as I the Lord your God am holy."

For a period of time, so as to allow the present situation to be clarified, perhaps there is wisdom in calling for an immediate and temporary moratorium on the use of the term *Holy* when applied to the land. The overuse of the term has caused it to be abused by certain communities and belief systems at the expense of others.

Abraham, the model of faith, sojourned in the land of Canaan as a guest and never owned land aside from the burial cave at Machpelah (Genesis 23:4–20), purchased at a fair price. Land is not to be confiscated or used to abuse people; justice is a norm in remaining obedient and faithful stewards of the land. In fact, continued possession of the land was conditional based on obedience to the Law. Israel's loss of the land and exile, first by Assyria in 721 B.C.E., and later by Babylon in 587–86 B.C.E., were interpreted by the prophets in these very terms.

Prophecies about the land and Israel's return to the land were scripturally applied to Jews who were exiles in Babylon. The book of Ezra describes the return to Israel and various prophets who anticipated it. These prophecies were fulfilled within the time of the initial return of the Jews as described in Ezra and are not intended to be projected to a time period beyond it.

From all that has been discussed, a final point concerning the land is that of the exclusive right or "divine claim" argument to the land that some faith communities claim. One of the great contemporary scholars of the concept of land in the Bible and ancient civilizations is W. D. Davies, Duke University professor emeritus of Old Testament. Professor Davies argues that Israel's relationship to the land is a "derived" relationship as a result of the covenant and Yahweh's grace. It is not a divine right nor a possession. Clearly the Hebrew people have a special attachment and history with this land, but so do Muslims and Christians. To grant to one community the divine "right" at the exclusion of another community is to miss the intent of the biblical message.

The consistent message of the Bible is that the people have been called to live in harmony with each other and be signs of Yahweh's blessings to the nations. (For a more complete development of the "land" concept see: Colin Chapman, *Whose Promised Land?* Lion Books, 1984; W. D. Davies, *The Territorial Dimension of Judaism,* University of

California Press, 1974; and the recently released *Who Are God's People in the Middle East?* by Gary Burge, Zondervan, 1993.)

Israel and the Future

In Jesus' day, as in ours, there was heightened expectation that the end of history was at hand. Many Jewish Zealots wished to overthrow the Romans as had the Maccabees two centuries before them, and usher in the final age. But Jesus always cautioned against using political actions, or the interpretation of certain signs, as having a future prophetic value. While he clearly stated "the end will come," (Matthew 24:14), he taught this concept in terms of the necessity of faith and obedience today. He told the disciples in the same passage: "But of that day and hour no one knows" (v. 36, RSV).

The same topic came up at the last moment of Jesus' earthly ministry, just prior to his ascension [Acts 1: 6–8]. Imagine yourself as one of the disciples who had been with Jesus through thick-and-thin times. This moment is your last opportunity for instructions before the ministry is turned over to you. You would, no doubt, have a multitude of serious questions to raise before Jesus leaves.

As they were gathering on the Mount of Olives overlooking Jerusalem, the disciples asked Jesus: "Lord, will you at this time restore the kingdom to Israel?" This is the Zealot's question about the future restoration of the Jews in a state within Palestine, a topic discussed constantly as they lived under Roman occupation. But here it was as if the disciples were saying: "Lord, we found your teachings inspiring. The miracles were awesome. The Resurrection was outstanding. But now are you going to do the big one— restore Israel to power?"

Note the tone of Jesus' response, for he is very direct:

"It is not for you to know the times or seasons which the Father has fixed by his own authority." (Acts 1:7, RSV). In other words, don't use signs or Scriptures as a timetable for the last days. You cannot know these mysteries, and it is not the focus of faithful discipleship. Instead, Jesus says: "But you shall be my witnesses in Jerusalem and in all Judea and Samaria, and to the end of the earth"(v. 8).

The Greek word for "witness" used by Luke in writing Acts is *martyrion*, the root word for "martyr." In other words, we are called to be faithful unto death in our witness, even in the most difficult places. The Middle East today, including Jerusalem, Israel and Palestine, are among those difficult places.

Then, while they were pondering these things, Jesus vanished from their sight. The ministry was now their responsibility. Two angels called out to them in their state of shock: "Men of Galilee, why do you stand looking into heaven?" [Acts 1:11]. This text is further confirmation that we are not to be anticipating prophetic signs of the end but to be engaged in ministry NOW.

The reference to Jerusalem in Acts 1 is instructive for our purposes. Jerusalem, the city that killed the prophets and crucified Jesus, was a place that struck fear into the hearts of the first Christians. But it was into this difficult place that they were called by the Lord to go.

We are called to carry his message of love, justice, and salvation into the difficult cities and crises. And today, Jerusalem itself and the Gaza Strip are among those places. We are reminded that among the first believers were Arabs, as the Pentecost account in Acts 2:11 mentions. The church of Jesus Christ, born in Jerusalem and then carried to Judea, Samaria, Damascus, Egypt, and Lebanon, has been faithfully present in these places since the day of Pentecost and has remained in unbroken continuity since the days of the

Ascension and Pentecost. But this church is suffering today, and it calls us to stand with it.

To date, over fifty different peace proposals have been brought forth since World War I. All have failed. Some have tried to impose a solution on one party or the other, and they quickly became nonstarters. Others simply pushed too fast, and the wheels of the vehicle spun into irrelevance in a short time.

This fragile vehicle for peace (not yet a formal peace treaty) called the accord will inevitably become stuck and mired down at times. There will be political assassinations and terrorist bombings that will bring dark clouds of doom over the region. The cycle of retaliation and "the thousand eyes for one" spirit of revenge will reemerge with a vengeance. The entire process of the peace accord will be jeopardized. Days, even months of cynicism, darkness, and hopelessness will dominate.

When that happens, courageous Israeli and Palestinian leaders will bear the burden of getting this fragile vehicle moving again. They may come to us—not just our government but our religious leaders—and ask for help.

Will we be ready? Will we be willing?

Our Palestinian lawyer friend, Jonathan Kuttab, long a resident of Jerusalem and a veteran of many failed peacemaking attempts, spoke to our Evangelicals for Middle East Understanding delegation during the dark days of October 1992. Though spoken before this year's historic handshake, his words bear repeating.

> Before any solution is found for the question of Palestine, before all the political maneuvers and shuttle diplomacies

are engaged, there is one prerequisite: a healing of souls and a mending of broken bones on both sides. Yes, we the Palestinians are the weaker and more brutalized party on the surface, but our cousins, the Jews, still carry the scars of Anti-Semitism, which I remind you is a Western problem. This healing is only possible if we look deep into our hearts and discover a spiritual and moral healing and new meaning to our lives. We must be honest before our Creator in how we treat our neighbors, and beg forgiveness from each other.

We Christians have the resources in our faith and the model of Jesus Christ to risk taking the first step. Forgiveness is at the heart of our faith and the message of Jesus. His death and resurrection in this very city is our legacy, and we the Palestinian Church, must break down the dividing walls between Muslims and Jews and Christians.

But we need you to stand with us, to pray for us, to come over and be with us if you are called. May God give us the strength and the vision that we might be faithful to this high calling.

Amen.

A Chronology of the Israeli-Palestinian Conflict

1880s: Anti-Semitism in Europe gives rise to Zionist movements and causes Jewish leaders to seek a homeland for Jews.

1896: Theodor Herzl publishes *Der Judenstaat* calling for a Jewish state, Palestine one of many options.

1897 (August): Herzl convenes the First Zionist Congress (Basel).

1901: World Zionist Organization establishes the Jewish National Fund to finance and purchase land in Palestine for exclusively Jewish colonization. Population of Palestine approximately 500,000 with 94% Palestinian Arab (Christian and Muslim), Jews 5%.

1914: Arabs in greater Syria (Syria, Lebanon, Palestine) protest Ottoman rule and demand independence. Outbreak of World War I.

1915: Sir Henry MacMahon, British high commissioner in Egypt, writes six letters to the sharif of Mecca, promising independent Arab States.

1916: Britain and France secretly sign the Sykes-Picot agreement providing for division of the Middle East between the two powers.

1917: Arab Legion and British Army enter Palestine; Palestinians request independence promised in MacMahon correspondence.

1917 (November): British Foreign Secretary Lord Arthur Balfour declares in a letter to Lord Rothschild that Britain will use its influence to establish in Palestine "national home to the Jewish people." The population of Palestine is 700,000, of whom 574,000 are Muslims, 70,000 Christians, and 56,000 Jews.

1919: Palestinians convene their first national conference with the goal of opposing the Balfour Declaration and establishing a Palestinian state.

1920: San Remo Conference grants Britain the Mandate for Syria and Lebanon.

1921: President Wilson of the United States sends the King-Crane Commission to investigate and report on the situation in Palestine; it recommends a secular democracy.

1922: British issue a white paper that rejects Palestinian independence and calls for a partition of the country. British census puts Palestinian Christian population in Jerusalem at 14,699 or 51% of Jerusalem's 28,607 inhabitants.

1929: The Jewish National Fund purchases a large section of land from an absentee Lebanese landowner; rioting occurrs with 116 Palestinian Arabs and 135 Jews killed.

1931: Britain investigates and publishes a new white paper, curbing land sales to Zionists and limiting immigration.

1936: Pogroms against Jews in Nazi German convinces British to raise quotas; full-scale Palestinian strikes lead to the outbreak of a rebellion that continued until 1939.

1937: British Royal (Peel) Commission concludes "the situation in Palestine has reached a deadlock" and calls for a partition of the country. Both sides reject the proposal.

1939–45: World War II and Nazi genocide against Jews. Massive Jewish immigration begins, many Western nations refuse Jews entry to their countries.

1942: Zionist Biltmore Declaration calls for unlimited Jewish settlement; rejects Palestinian self-determination.

1945–47: Zioenst paramilitary groups the Haganah, Irgun, and Stern Gang launch bloody campaign against British and Palestinians.

1947 (**November 29**): The UN approves the partition plan. Palestinian Arabs own 92% of the land and represent 67% of population, but UN partition proposes 55% of state to Jews.

1948: British announce intent to leave Palestine on May 15, 1948. On April 8, an Irgun terrorist unit attacks the village of Deir Yassin near Jerusalem, where 254 Palestinians are killed. Red Cross investigator condemns the massacres. Eventually 750-770,000 Palestinian refugees leave for neighboring Arab countries.

1949 (**December**): UN Resolution 194 calls for the return of Palestinian refugees to their homes.

1951: Jordan's King Abdullah killed after leaving Jerusalem's Mosque of Omar. On December 25 (Christmas Day), Palestinian Christian villages Ikrit and Biram destroyed.

1956: Suez Crisis: Israel, France, and Britain invade Egypt. President Eisenhower opposes invasion and war is averted.

1957: Arab League announces boycott of companies dealing with Israel until Palestinian rights are adopted.

1964 (May 28): Palestine Liberation Organization established in Jerusalem, joins Arab League.

1967 (June): Israel defeats Egypt, Syria, and Jordan and occupies the Golan Heights, East Jerusalem, West Bank, Gaza Strip, and Sinai Peninsula. UN Resolution 242 adopted.

1969: February 1-4, Palestine National Council (PNC) elects Yasser Arafat chairman, reiterates call for secular, democratic state and equality for all citizens.

1973: On January 12, the Eleventh PNC calls for independent Palestinian state on any portion of historic Palestine.

1976: On April 12, first (and only) free municipal elections in Occupied Territories bring twenty-five nationalist candidates.

1977: Likud party comes to power under Menachem Begin. On November 9, Egyptian President Sadat visits Israel. On December 25, Israel's Knesset declares it illegal to proselytize Jews.

1978: Israel invades Southern Lebanon on March 14 and occupies Lebanon to the Litani River.

1978: Soviet-U.S. peace talks, based on UN Resolutions 242 and 338 (land exchanged for peace) fail in Geneva.

1979: Camp David Peace Accord signed in Washington, D.C. among the United States, Israel, and Egypt.

1980: European Economic Community issues Venice Declaration calling for end to Israeli settlements and accepting Israeli and Palestinian rights to self-determination.

1982 (June): Israel invades Lebanon in its "Peace for Galilee" campaign. Sabra-Shatila massacre September 16-18. Approximately 400,000 Israelis protest in Tel Aviv.

1983: UN General Assembly adopts Resolution 38/58c, calling for international peace conference, with Israel and PLO to negotiate self-determination and independent states for each and Israeli withdrawal to pre-1967 borders in exchange for security guarantees.

1987 (December): Palestinian Intifada begins and spreads throughout occupied West Bank and Gaza Strip.

1988: Over 225 Palestinians killed in first five months of Intifada. November 15, PNC declares independence and calls for Palestinian state beside Israel, based on U.N. resolutions. On December 7 in Stockholm, Arafat meets delegation of five U.S.-Jewish leaders and recognizes Israel.

1990 (August): Iraq invades Kuwait.

1991 (January): Coalition of UN armies attack Iraq, forcing its defeat and withdrawal from Kuwait.

1992: Madrid peace talks begin. Israel receives ten billion in loan guarantees from the U.S.

1993: U.S.-sponsored peace talks stall in Washington after ninth and tenth round. (September) Israel and PLO recognize each other and begin transitional Palestinian government in Jericho and Gaza.

Blessed Are the Peacemakers

You can be a peacemaker in the Holy Land through Mercy Corps International. Your donation will help bring peace to families who are suffering in the very land where Jesus shared his redemptive message of salvaton.

Jobs are being created, medical help is being provided, and villages are being reconstructed. Mercy Corps is building confidence—and hope—for the future.

Your donation will help us continue this important work in the Holy Land. Call in your pledge to 1-800-292-2355, or send your check to:

Mercy Corps International
P. O. Box 9
Portland, OR 97207-0009

As a reminder to pray for the peace of Jerusalem, you will receive an olive wood cross from the Holy Land for your donation of $15 or more.

Dan O'Neill, Co-founder
Don Wagner, Director of Middle East Programs

Mercy Corps International is a member of ECFA, is registered with the Council of Better Business Bureaus, is a member of InterAction, and was rated sixth in the nation among all relief and development organizations in its use of funds (*Money* magazine, December 1992). Donations are tax deductible to the extent allowed by law.